RSV COMMENTARY

An Exposition on the Book of Ephesians

RANDY VANCE JR

WESTBOW
PRESS®
A DIVISION OF THOMAS NELSON
& ZONDERVAN

WestBow Press books may be ordered through booksellers or by contacting:

WestBow Press
A Division of Thomas Nelson & Zondervan
1663 Liberty Drive
Bloomington, IN 47403
www.westbowpress.com
1 (866) 928-1240

ISBN: 978-1-9736-0308-5 (sc)
ISBN: 978-1-9736-0309-2 (hc)
ISBN: 978-1-9736-0307-8 (e)

Library of Congress Control Number: 2017914862

Print information available on the last page.

WestBow Press rev. date: 9/26/2017

Introduction

The Book of Ephesians

It is believed that Priscilla and Aquila were the first to bring the gospel to the Ephesians. Paul wrote the letter to the Ephesians from prison in Rome in AD 64, which we can read in Acts 20–27. Tychicus was the one who brought Paul's letter to the Ephesians. It is probable that the letter was circulated for all the churches in that area to read.

In the Bible, the first three chapters of the book of Ephesians deal with doctrine, which is Paul's usual practice (Galatians, Philippians, and Thessalonians). The last three chapters deal with application. It's kind of like being in school. You learn math, reading, and English so you can apply them in life. So it is with the Word of God: you read and apply it to life. Some may say, "Well, the Word of God is not relevant to today's time." In the past, some people didn't think learning English and math was relevant to life. It wasn't until you moved into the world that you applied those things. That's the way it is with the Word of God. We should apply it to our daily lives.

The book of Ephesians is written to believers, just as Paul's other letters.

Ephesians Chapter 1

Chapters 1–3 are doctrinal. Greetings can be found in Ephesians 1:1–2. Paul's praise to God for His spiritual blessings—chosen, predestined, redeemed, and inheritance—are covered in verses 3–14. Paul's first prayer for the Ephesians—knowledge of hope of His calling, riches of His glory, and greatness of His power—can be found in verses 15–23.

Paul begins his letter with who he is: "Paul an apostle of Jesus Christ by the will of God" (Eph. 1:1). This was a normal practice for Paul. He did the same in the books of Romans, Corinthians, Galatians, Colossians, and Timothy. An apostle is one who is sent forth as an ambassador, a messenger, or a delegate. This ambassador carries a message from the country he or she represents and has the authority of that country's ruler.

In Acts chapter 9, we can read about how Paul became an apostle. There are several requirements for someone to be considered to be an apostle. They had to see the resurrected Christ and be chosen by Christ Himself. They had to perform miracles to prove they were apostles, and they founded churches. I seriously doubt many of today's preachers are apostles in the New Testament sense. They haven't seen the resurrected Christ. For Matthias to become an apostle, he had to see the resurrected Christ. He took Judas Iscariot's place, and we can read that account in Acts 1:22–26. Paul defended his apostleship in 2 Corinthians chapter 12.

Paul said he was an apostle of Jesus Christ. He wasn't an ambassador of the emperor or some king, but of Jesus Christ. Christ sent him to the church in Ephesus. He was Christ's messenger to them, as well as to the Gentiles. *Jesus* means "Jehovah is salvation," "or Jehovah saved." *Christ* means Messiah or Anointed. In other words, Jesus is the anointed

1

one for individuals to be saved by the Lord. Paul mentions he is an apostle by the will of God. This was neither his choice nor the choice of the Sanhedrin. If he or the Sanhedrin had anything to do with it, he would not have been an apostle of Jesus Christ. He would have been the ambassador or delegate of Jerusalem to do harm to the Christian churches, as he started out doing. So it was the will, or desire, of God to make him an apostle. It was God's choice to make him His ambassador. Now he had the message and authority from Jesus Christ.

Next, Paul mentions to whom the letter is addressed: "To the saints which are in Ephesus, and to the faithful in Christ Jesus" (Eph. 1:1). This letter is not addressed to all citizens in Ephesus. Paul is writing this letter to the ones who are separated from sin and set apart by God. In other words, this letter is written to Christians. Saints are literally holy ones. They are set apart by Christ. This letter is addressed to the church in Ephesus.

Ephesus was the capital city in Asia Minor. It was once called the first and greatest city of Asia. It was the place of the temple of Diana, who was a Roman goddess, also known as the temple of Artemis, who was a Greek god. The temple is considered one of the seven wonders of the ancient world. Interestingly, the temple was a bank, a place for criminals to hide, a place to worship Diana, and a museum for paintings. Ephesus was also known for its theater, which was the largest in the world and seated fifty thousand people. Aquila and Priscilla were left in the city by Paul to work, Timothy was a bishop at the church, Trophimus was a native and Tychicus was sent to Ephesus (Acts 20:4, 20:29; 2 Tim. 4:12). Paul served there for three years. The apostle John was a pastor, and he wrote a letter to them in Revelation chapter 2. Today, the city is empty except for a little Turkish village called Ayasaluk.

Paul's letter in the book of Ephesians is addressed to the believers in Christ Jesus. This does not mean that saints and the faithful are two different things. They are the holy ones and believers in Christ Jesus. So in other words, they are the same things. We can go back to Acts 19:1–20:38 to see the faithful. The ones who believed came, confessed, and showed their deeds. They burned the books containing formulas for their magic; they did this so people could see they believed in Christ. So Paul is writing to the ones who are the faithful in Christ, who have turned from their sins to Christ. They are considered holy ones and saints.

Paul moves on from the introduction of this letter to greetings. He says, "Grace be unto you, and peace, from God our Father, and from the Lord Jesus Christ" (Eph. 1:2). Grace typically means unmerited favor, and peace is rest. This is a normal benediction from Paul. He says grace and peace in his letters to the Romans, Corinthians, Galatians, Philippians, Colossians, and Thessalonians; he also uses this greeting in his letter to Philemon. Notice Paul says peace and grace from God our Father and from the Lord Jesus Christ. That is where grace and peace come from. Grace, again, is unmerited favor. No matter how much we do, we cannot receive grace from God by doing good works or deeds.

For the Ephesians to be "who they were in Christ" means that God had to show them grace or favor. Knowing they were sinful people worshipping a false god, the one true God could have left them in that condition. But no, God showed them grace. And it's by His grace that they are saved. Peace is rest, being reconciled to God through the shed blood of Jesus Christ. We have unmerited favor and rest from God and from the Lord Jesus Christ. Grace comes from God and from Jesus, and to have rest is to be reconciled by God and by Jesus. *Lord* means supreme in authority. And to say Lord Jesus Christ is to say that Jesus is supreme in authority and that He is Jehovah's anointed for people to be saved by God. Everything is placed under the feet of Jesus, which gives Him the title Lord. And we'll look at that later.

"Blessed be the God and Father of our Lord Jesus Christ, who hath blessed us with all spiritual blessings in heavenly places in Christ" (Eph. 1:3). Paul praises God the Father of our Lord Jesus Christ. The word *blessed* here means to speak well of and be worthy of praise. God is to be praised for what He has done through Jesus Christ. God and God alone is to be praised for His blessings. We're not talking about blessings as far as material things are concerned. Yes, God is to be praised for His blessings on our lives, but more importantly, He should be praised for His blessings on us for salvation. Paul is acknowledging God, who has blessed them with all spiritual blessings. To be who they were in Christ, all praise goes to God.

Notice Paul says, "God and Father of our Lord Jesus Christ." Even though Jesus is the Son of God, God is the God of Jesus when Jesus became man. Paul is speaking well or giving praise to God the Father of our Lord Jesus. In the gospel of John, Jesus refers to God as His Father several times (John 10:29–30, 20:17). Paul mentions this in some of his other letters as well (Rom. 15:6; 2 Cor. 11:31). This shows the unity of God the Father and of Jesus Christ. Even though Jesus is Lord, He is under God, who is His Father. All blessing and praise goes to God for His grace and peace.

God has blessed the Ephesian Church with all spiritual blessing. The word *blessed* here means to give favor upon someone. This is every blessing with which God has blessed them. Again, it is not material blessing; it is spiritual blessing. It is salvation. That which is spiritual is noncarnal, meaning not of this world and coming from the Holy Spirit. The word *blessings*, the third time Paul uses the term, means benefits. It is God the Father who gives favor upon us with spiritual benefits. Everything that is needed for our salvation, God has blessed us with. That should be more important than having material things.

For Abraham, God's benefit was to be a blessed nation (Gen. 12:2–3), and all nations have been blessed through Abraham's seed (Gen. 22:18), who is Jesus Christ. God blessed Jabez, who was more honorable than his brothers (1 Chron. 4:10). The nation of Israel was blessed by God (Isa. 61:9). All these blessings from God are of His work alone, and He should be the one who gets the praise. "In heavenly places" literally means in the heavenlies—the place where Christ is seated and the right hand of God, which is the place of authority. All spiritual blessings come from God, but they are through Christ. In other words, our salvation is through Jesus Christ our Lord. Who we are in Christ is through Him. Without Christ, we would not have the spiritual blessings.

"According as He hath chosen us in Him before the foundation of the world" (Eph. 1:4). Being chosen "before the foundation of the world" means God picked out or selected them before He even laid down the world—from eternity. Before God created the heavens and the earth, He had already chosen people for Himself. What does this mean for us? It means that believers in Christ have been chosen or selected by God for Himself. We don't know whom God has chosen, and it is not our position to decide who is chosen. We are commanded to go out into the world and make disciples (Matt. 28:19).

We cannot comprehend eternity. God said to Moses that He is the I AM. He always exists. In Revelation, Jesus tells John that He is the Alpha and the Omega, the beginning and the end, and the first and the last (Rev. 1:8, 11). Just as God has always existed, so does Jesus Christ. They always existed before time began, and they will always exist even when time ends. God has chosen people for Himself before the laying down of the world. God had in mind the plan of salvation before the foundation of the world.

Chosen is a scriptural term. The word is taught or found throughout the Old and New Testaments. It is in Deuteronomy 7:6, Isaiah 45:4, and John 6:44, just to name a few. God chose us for Himself, and Paul tells us why in Ephesians 1:6.

"That we should be holy and without blame before Him in love" (Eph. 1:4). God has chosen them so they would be holy and blameless. To be holy is to be set apart. It is to be set apart from sin and set apart to God. What does it mean to be holy? Our calling is a holy calling (2 Tim. 1:9). It is a calling unlike any other calling. Our calling is to salvation through Jesus Christ. Our calling is to be set apart from sin and to God. God has called us from uncleanness (1 Thess. 4:7), we have been called according to His purpose (Rom. 8:28), and we have been redeemed from all iniquity for good works (Titus 2:14). Paul told the Colossians that they are holy and beloved (Col. 3:12), and just as they are such, so should we be. To be holy is to live a life that is different.

People should be able to see a difference between believers and nonbelievers. God chose us for Himself so we should be holy. If our calling is a holy calling, if we are called from uncleanness, if we have been called according to His purpose, and if we are redeemed from all iniquity, then why do we continue to live as if we are not holy? Our lives should demonstrate that we are holy. That doesn't mean we should live with a self-righteous type of attitude, but rather that we should live in a way that others can tell a difference. We shouldn't go around passing judgment on others who live in sin. Neither should we be like the Pharisee who thanked God that he wasn't like other men who are sinners. But we should give God praise for setting us apart from our sin and to Him.

Not only should they be holy, but they also should be blameless. They are to be without fault or flaw. Not that they will not sin for all sin, but they should not be living a life contrary to holiness. As chosen by God, they are blameless before Him. This means they are holy and blameless in His presence. There is only one way that can be, and that is in Christ. It is only through Christ that they and we can be holy and blameless.

We can be blameless when we stand before Christ on that last day (1 Cor. 1:8). We are blameless by the death of Christ (Col. 1:22). It was His shed blood that was without blemish or spot and can make us unblemished and without spot (1 Pet. 1:19). And we need to be diligent that we may be found in Him without spot and blameless (2 Pet. 3:14). Just as we are set apart for God, meaning our lives are different, so it is to be without blame or fault. We should not continue to live in sin. Yes, we will sin, but we will not be habitual sinners. God did not choose us before the foundation of the world so we would stay the same. No, He chose us for Himself to be holy and without blame. This is one part of our spiritual blessings in Christ.

"Having predestinated us unto the adoption of children by Jesus Christ to Himself" (Eph. 1:5). God has chosen them before the foundation of the world to be holy and blameless, so in love He has predetermined them to be placed as sons by Christ to Himself. When Paul wrote that God predestinated us, he is saying that God predetermined—that is, determined in advance—to the adoption of children by Jesus Christ. Predestinated is also another biblical term and it has also created some problems by people who take words and abuse them. Here it means that God has predetermined to adopt us by Jesus Christ. So, if He has chosen us before the foundation of the world, then He predetermined how He was going to do it.

Adoption means that a child belongs to a family. God predetermined to adopt us into His family. Just as a family predetermines to adopt a child and call that child their own, so does God. Since we are adopted, we are sons of God, and now we can call God Abba Father, as Paul put it to the Galatians (Gal. 4:6). The predetermination is according to His pleasure in Ephesians 1:11. And whom He foreknew He predetermined to be conformed to the image of His Son (Rom. 8:28).

Our salvation is from God, and the how is "according to the good pleasure of His will" (Eph. 1:5). Good pleasure is the same as to seem well, to think it good. So, it seemed well to God, and He thought it was good that He predetermined us to be placed as sons of God through Jesus Christ. In other words, nothing else seemed good to God than our salvation. God thought it good for us to be children of God through Jesus Christ, and it is through faith in Him.

False religions make you work for your salvation and just hope it was good enough. God did not think that would be good. He already said our righteousness is like a filthy rag (Isa. 64:6). It was not good for us to work for our salvation, and working for our salvation would not accomplish anything. To be adopted into a family does not mean that a child must be good enough for that family. That family adopts and loves that child. If a child must work to be accepted by a family, then that family does not love that child.

Wouldn't you say that about false religions that make you work for salvation? What does that say about a god who makes you work to be good enough? If you must work for your salvation, is it worth the trouble? Can you have peace knowing that all you have done might not be good enough? Can you call it grace if you must work for it? God sent His Son because He loved the world (John 3:16). God thought it was good to send His Son and that through Him we might be children of God. This is the other part of God's spiritual blessings on us.

Paul said this is "to the praise of the glory of His grace, wherein He hath made us accepted in the Beloved" (Eph. 1:6). This is the reason God would bless us: so that in turn we would praise Him. His spiritual blessings are His choosing us to be holy and blameless and predetermining us to be adopted by Jesus Christ. The praise is of the glory, which is honor of His grace. That is favor. We cannot earn this favor to be chosen and adopted. We do not have God's favor on us because of our looks, ability, or heritage. God's grace is unmerited and undeserved. We praise Him for His grace, which He freely bestowed on us. God chose to honor us with His blessings in the Beloved, which is a title for Jesus Christ. So we can say with the hymn writer, praise God from whom all blessings flow; praise Him all creatures here below; praise Him above, ye heavenly host; Praise Father, Son, and Holy Ghost. Amen.

"In whom we have redemption through His blood" (Eph. 1:7). Continuing, Paul says in the Beloved we have redemption through His blood. Redemption is ransom paid in full; the blood of Jesus Christ is the ransom paid in full. Jesus said He gave His life as a ransom (Matt. 20:28). There is not enough money to pay this ransom price. No amount of good deeds can pay this ransom price. The price for sin was the shedding of blood. The writer of Hebrews said, "for it is not possible that the blood of bulls and of goats should take away sins" (Heb. 10:4). The blood of animals could not remove what Christ did on the cross. The only payment that could redeem us was the blood of Christ.

Paul also said that the through the blood of Christ they have "forgiveness of sins" (Eph. 1:7). It is the blood of Jesus Christ that pardons the prisoner. The pardoned prisoner is considered not guilty and is to be freed from punishment. So, not only do they have redemption through His blood, but also forgiveness of sins. That goes for us as well. So what we have here is a former prisoner set free by the ransom price paid by Christ; we are no longer considered guilty for our sin, and we are free from the punishment that came along with sin.

Sin is a sideslip. That is, to fall aside or to lapse or deviate from the truth. It is as if a warrior intentionally fell upon his enemy, which indicates reckless and willful sin. It is considered falling down where one should have stood upright. Sin is called a trespass, slip, or a fault. That is, to sin is to be deliberate and intentional. So, with sin comes with guilt and punishment. And to be forgiven is to be set free from the guilt and punishment of sin. To be in bondage to sin is to be deliberately living in it. Christ paid the required price to set us free, and to remain as a prisoner is to continue to live in a prison with the doors open.

When Christ paid the price, we were freed from the guilt and punishment of our trespasses, the willful and intentional sin. In Psalms, David wrote, "Blessed is he whose transgression is forgiven, whose sin is covered" (32:1). That is, how happy is the man whose rebellion is taken away. Paul said the same thing in Romans 4:7. The writer of Hebrews also said God will no more remember their sins and iniquities (Heb.

10:17). The blood of Christ is what freed us from our sins and forgives us of our sins.

Paul said that all this is "according to the riches of His grace" (Eph. 1:7). It is the wealth of God's undeserved favor that they can be redeemed and forgiven. That wealth of grace extends to our day in time. God's grace will never run out. That doesn't mean we should take advantage of His grace. Or, as Paul put it, frustrate the grace of God (Gal. 2:21). It means we should never disesteem God's favor. It's amazing that even though we lived in sin, God was willing to show us grace. Even though we were slaves to sin, God was willing to place us as children. Even though we were sinners, God predetermined to make us holy and without blame. This is according to the wealth of His favor. We shouldn't disesteem or think less of God's grace by continuing to live in sin. Again, nothing we could have done or who we are, just God's favor.

"Wherein He hath abounded toward us in all wisdom and prudence" (Eph. 1:8). It is His grace that He made to exceed or overflow toward the Ephesians. Even knowing who they were, God's grace overflowed toward them. Knowing who we were, God's grace overflowed toward us too. How many people would be willing to show us grace if we abused it? Think about someone with an abundance of wealth; do you think they will waste it on someone who treats their favor with disgust? I don't think so. But God's grace was overflowing. Remember, this was written to believers, and so Paul reminds them that God is wealthy in His grace, and His grace overflowed toward them and us. The grace of God should never be a license to sin.

Wisdom is the insight, and prudence is understanding. That is, God had the wisdom to plan to redeem mankind and the prudence to make it happen. It was God's wisdom that He planned for redemption to come through Christ, and His prudence made it happen. It is God's grace that overflowed toward us that we have redemption and forgiveness. Paul said to the Corinthians that the preaching of Christ's crucifixion is the wisdom of God (1 Cor. 1:23–24). Some think it was foolish for God to do that. But remember, God thought it was good that He would do that.

"Having made known to us the mystery of His will" (Eph. 1:9). Mystery is knowledge withheld, and God's will is His desire or determination. This mystery is not like the plot of a book or a movie that you try to figure out before the end. This secret is not something that only a select few can know. This is not some secret society that you must join in order to know the secrets. God's secret, or knowledge, that He withheld is something the He chose to withhold until He decided to reveal it. God chose to reveal His desire to us "according to His good pleasure which He hath purposed in Himself" (Eph. 1:9). Here is the term *good pleasure* again. It seems well, or He thought it would be good. So, it is according to what He thought would be good that we should know what His purpose was.

That which He purposed is what He planned beforehand. God thought it would be good and planned beforehand to make known knowledge previously withheld. In other words, the people of old did not know God's plan of salvation. All the things in the law were only a foreshadowing of things to come. They didn't know that what they did in the temple was only temporary. He did not reveal His plan to them. The prophets foretold of the coming Messiah, but they didn't know of God's plan for Him.

For God to plan beforehand to reveal His will meant that He also planned beforehand who He would choose to write down His will. God would eventually make known the secret of His desire in His written Word. God thought it would be good and planned beforehand to make known to us His will. Paul told the Colossians that He revealed His will to the saints (Col. 1:26). How can we know God's will? By reading His Word. He chose to reveal His will so that we would know. God did not leave us wondering how we should live. He did not leave us wondering how to have salvation. He reveals His plan to us in the Word of God.

"That in the dispensation of the fulness of times He might gather together in one all things in Christ, both which are in heaven, and which are on earth; even in Him" (Eph. 1:10). This is in view of the stewardship of the completion of time. Dispensation is administration, managing, or stewardship. It is like managing a household or a business. Someone who is a steward or who manages a company is managing time, resources, and expenses. But in a family, the husband or wife manages time, money, errands, and, of course, the family members.

Here God is managing resources, time, and people. In other words, God had a set time that He would send Christ. In God's management,

He arranged for all things to work according to His plan. So when the time came, He completed salvation by Christ's death on the cross. Nothing changed in God's plan for sending His Son. He set the right time, the right place, and the right people for Him to come. When man sinned in the garden, it didn't throw off God's plan. When Israel was in captivity, it didn't set back His plan. When people demanded that Christ be crucified, it didn't stress God. It was God's plan to send Christ at the right time and place and to use the right people. That's God's dispensation.

Paul said that Christ might gather together into one all things in Him. God will head up, or unite, all things under one head, and that head is Christ. At the set time, God sent His Son, and at the set time, God will unite all things in heaven and on earth. God's management of time did not stop at the cross; it continues until the final day, when all things will be united under Christ. There will be peace, and Christ will reign.

"In whom also we have obtained an inheritance" (Eph. 1:11). Paul is letting them know what else they have in Christ. Inheritance is something allotted to somebody. In Israel's early days, the people received their lands by lots, kind of like throwing dice. They would throw pebbles, and however they landed, the land in question would be assigned to that tribe. They went in a certain order when allotting the land. They would not choose what land would be theirs, and they did not choose who would receive the land in question. In a will, a testator leaves certain things to certain people based on his or her choice. In Israel, the people went in a prescribed order, and when the first tribe cast the lot, they would receive the land indicated by the throw, and then it would continue until the land had been allotted to all the tribes except for the Levites.

Here, Paul is saying that in Christ we were made a heritage. We were made a heritage through Christ. In other words, we are counted with Israel. In Deuteronomy 4:20; 9:29; and 32:9, Israel was made to be God's inheritance. But because of Christ's death on the cross, believers are now made to be God's inheritance also. Paul said to the Colossians, "giving thanks unto the Father, which hath made us meet to be partakers of the inheritance of the saints in light" (Col. 1:12). Paul is giving thanks to God for qualifying us to be partakers of the inheritance. He did not leave us to try to qualify ourselves to be His portion. In Christ we are qualified to be partakers. God did not cast lots to see who would be His inheritance. If that had been the case, who would be His? Christ qualified us and made us an inheritance.

"Being predestinated according to the purpose of Him who worketh all things after the counsel of His own will" (Eph. 1:11). Again, Paul mentions predestinate. God decided beforehand according to His intention. He made all things happen according to His determination of His own desire. Man did nothing in planning this. This was not a decision based on how good we were or where we came from. God's intention to make us an inheritance was God's plan, and He made it happen. We had nothing to do with it. God decided beforehand, long ago, to predestinate us to be an inheritance. So His plan lined up with His decision to make us a heritage in Christ. Throughout the ages, centuries, and millennia, His plan never changed. Isaiah said God's plans are fixed (Isa. 46:10). Adopted before the foundation of the world in Christ, accepted in the Beloved, redeemed and forgiven in Christ, made a heritage, has been God's plan and His good pleasure. Paul said to the Romans, "for who hath known the mind of the Lord? Or who hath been His counsellor" (Rom. 11:34)?

Worketh means to be active and operative. So all things are active and operative in line with His purpose of His own desire. It's like a blueprint: somebody had the idea and laid out the plans, and then the builders built it according to the designer's plans. God made us a heritage, which He decided beforehand and planned how He would do this, and everything lined up according to His plan. So everything is active and operative in line with His purpose, upon which He desired everything to operate.

When God created the heavens and the earth, everything He made worked the way He intended it to. This is God's providence in the world. God put men and women in the right place, where He desired them to be. So it is with our salvation. God has orchestrated everything to work the way He intended for our salvation. He sent Christ at the right time, and His death, burial, and resurrection happened at the right time; God sent men and women to spread the gospel in line with His plan; and at the right time, God's plan included our salvation. We were predetermined to be made a heritage in Christ in line with God's plan, and everything worked out the way He intended. Everything has gone according to plan.

"That we should be to the praise of His glory, who first trusted in Christ" (Eph. 1:12). The ones who first trusted in Christ should be to the praise of His glory. It was the Jews who first hoped in Christ, and that was God's intention. Salvation came through the Jewish people, which was God's plan and desire. It was the Jews who were first predestined to be God's inheritance. They are God's chosen people, and it was the Jews who first had opportunity to come to salvation through Christ. All praise should be to His honor for what He has done. We honor God by praising Him. The believing Jews were the first to praise God for His salvation, but His plan did not stop with them.

"In whom ye also trusted, after that ye heard the word of truth, the gospel of your salvation" (Eph. 1:13). Paul now goes from the believing Jews trusting in Christ to the Ephesian believers. The same Christ who the Jews trusted, or in which they hoped, is the same Christ who the Ephesians trusted. The Jews trusted in Christ long before the Ephesians or Gentiles. In other words, the Jews heard of the coming Messiah long before He came. God spoke to the Jews through His prophets. It was also God's intention for the Gentiles to trust in Christ. He predetermined to give salvation to the Gentiles through Christ, as He had for the Jews. The Gentiles have the same opportunity for salvation.

After they heard the word of truth, they trusted in Christ. *Word* is something spoken, and *truth* is something that is not concealing. God did not hide the truth that we needed a Savior. God did not hide the truth that we are sinners. Neither did He hide the truth of how to be saved. Faith comes by hearing and hearing by the Word of God, Paul told the Romans (Rom. 10:17). So here they believed because they heard the word of truth. Somebody had to bring the Word to the Ephesians, and that somebody may have been Aquila and Priscilla. Salvation comes by hearing the Word of God proclaimed. James wrote that His own will begat us with the word of truth (James 1:18). The word of truth is the same as the Word of God.

Paul said the word of truth is the gospel of your salvation. The gospel is the good news, and it is the good news of your salvation. In the book of Mark, Jesus said, "Go ye into all the world, and preach the gospel to every creature. He that beleiveth and is baptized shall be saved; but he that beleiveth not shall be damned" (16:16). The gospel is Jesus's life, death, burial, and resurrection. The gospel tells us how we can have salvation; that's why it's called the gospel of your salvation. After they heard the gospel, they trusted in Christ and are now saved and delivered from their sin.

"In whom also after that ye believed, ye were sealed with that Holy Spirit of promise" (Eph. 1:13). When they believed in Christ, the Holy Spirit sealed them. When something is sealed, it is stamped with a signet. A king would stamp the wax seal of an official letter with his ring. The stamp is for security, ownership, authenticity, and authority. Sealed by the Holy Spirit means they are safe and secure in Christ. It does not mean that they did not have difficulties in life, but their salvation was secure. The seal of the Holy Spirit means God owns them. That is, He purchased us through Christ.

Paul said the Holy Spirit is the promise, which is an announcement for a pledge. God made the promise in Joel 2:28 that He would pour His Spirit upon all flesh. Jesus said that He would send the promise of His Father (Luke 24:49). The promise was fulfilled on the day of Pentecost (Acts 2). Paul wrote to the Galatians that "the blessing of Abraham might come on the Gentiles through Jesus Christ; that we might receive the promise of the Spirit through faith" (Gal. 3:14). The blessing is salvation by faith. Abraham believed God, and it was counted to him as righteousness (Gen. 15:6), and we can have that same blessing— salvation—when we believe in Jesus Christ. But we also receive the promise of the Spirit through faith. Paul is saying that when we believe, we receive the promise of the Holy Spirit. Abraham did not have the promise of the Holy Spirit. The promise of the Holy Spirit as the seal means that we are safe, secure, owned, and authentic, and that God has authority in our lives.

"Which is the earnest of our inheritance until the redemption of the purchased possession" (Eph. 1:14). In this verse, Paul says that the Holy Spirit is the down payment, earnest money, guarantee, or deposit of our inheritance. Earnest has also been called an engagement ring. The Holy

Spirit is not only the promise that we are God's people; it is also earnest money that God will fulfill His promise. This down payment doesn't end when hard times come and our faith is put to the test. Neither does it end when we die. The Holy Spirit of promise is God's promise to us; the Holy Spirit is our guarantee until the day of redemption. It is just like when a man gives an engagement ring to the woman he loves; it means he promises to take her as his wife on the day they have set. God has set that day of redemption, and His Spirit is that engagement ring, or guarantee, that we will be delivered. We can rest assured that God's promises are not like our promises. Some people make promises that are soon forgotten, but not God. God's plan included the Holy Spirit of promise. Earnest money is promising to finish the transaction. We may say that God is delaying His promise or that He forgot, but remember: His promise is there until the day of redemption or until the day of our deliverance.

The Holy Spirit is God's promise that we are His inheritance, or heritage. When people write wills, they have them notarized, which signifies that what is mentioned within them will stand. So whoever was promised something in the will, the person who made the will planned it. Those people become the legal inheritors of whatever is mention in the will. We became the legal inheritors through Christ. Since we are adopted into the family of God, we have an inheritance. God gave us His Holy Spirit as the down payment, and He will fulfill His promise. This promise is good until the day of redemption of the purchased possession.

Redemption is deliverance. Redemption in Ephesians 1:7 was a ransom from the bondage of sin, a release from sin. This redemption is being freed from our present bodies. This redemption completes the ransom. This redemption is deliverance from this earth. No matter how long we live, God's promise remains until that final day when we are in His presence.

Purchased possession is something acquired; it is also known as a peculiar possession. God purchased us with the blood of Christ (Acts 20:28). Peter said we are a peculiar people (1 Pet. 2:9), not that we are strange but that we have been purchased. We are God's possession, and rest assured, God will never forget His promises in Christ. God's predetermined plan is according to His desire, and He is working everything to the way He planned. All this Paul says is "unto the praise of His glory" (Eph. 1:14). Everything He promised with His Spirit will be to the glory of God.

"Wherefore I also, after I heard of your faith in the Lord Jesus, and love unto all the saints" (Eph. 1:15). Now we move on to Paul's prayer for the Ephesian believers. Paul heard of their faith in Jesus Christ. Some have translated this phrase as "I heard the faith, which is among you." Paul had spent some years at the church in Ephesus (Acts 19:8–10), and the way he said this seems like he was a stranger to them. Remember, Paul is in prison, and somebody had to bring him word of the Ephesians trusting in Jesus as Lord and Savior, word not only of their salvation but also their love for the saints, or holy ones. This has also been translated as "the love which is toward all the saints." Because of their faith in the Lord Jesus, they showed love toward all the saints.

Because of their faith and love, Paul says that he would "cease not to give thanks for you, making mention of you in my prayers" (Eph. 1:16). This is considered one of Paul's prison prayers. This is the first in the book of Ephesians, with the second one appearing in chapter 3. His prayers for other believers are also recorded in the books of Philippians and Colossians, both in chapter 1. When Paul prays, he remembers them, giving thanks for their faith in Christ and for their love toward the saints. His prayer was not for material things but for the believers. Even though he was in prison, he prayed for the Ephesians, Philippians, and Colossians. It is the habit of some to pray for lost souls and then forget them once they are saved. Paul continued to pray for them constantly. He continued to intercede for them. Even though Paul was in prison for no reason, that did not stop him from giving thanks for the believers.

"That the God of our Lord Jesus Christ, the Father of glory" (Eph. 1:17). The God of our Lord Jesus Christ means that God is also the God of Jesus. Jesus Himself called the Father, My God in Matthew 27:46. In John 20:17, Jesus said, "I ascend unto My Father, and your Father; and to My God, and your God." Jesus is not saying that there are two Fathers and two Gods but that Jesus's Father and God are the same Father and God to us. So Paul is saying that he is praying to the God of our Lord Jesus Christ, and He is our God also. There are not two Gods here but the same God, which we know is the same God of our Lord Jesus Christ. The Father of glory is the glorious Father. God is the Father of glory, which here means majesty. Paul is praying to God the Father of glory, or majesty. All glory and honor go to God for all He has done, from creation to salvation to eternity.

Paul is praying to God the Father that He "may give you the spirit of wisdom and revelation in the knowledge of Him" (Eph. 1:17). The spirit here is not the Holy Spirit. They already had the Spirit's indwelling when they trusted in Jesus Christ. Paul is praying that they would have complete wisdom and revelation in the knowledge of God. Wisdom comes from God, and it is pure, peaceable, gentle, easy to be entreated, full of mercy and good fruits, without partiality, and without hypocrisy (James 3:17). *Revelation* means uncovering or disclosure. The prayer is for God to give them the spirit of wisdom and revelation for the acknowledgement of Him. They cannot have wisdom and revelation without God giving it to them. James wrote, "if any of you lack wisdom, let him ask of God, that giveth to all men liberally, and upbraideth not; and it shall be given to him" (James 1:5). Basically, God gives us wisdom bountifully and does not rebuke us for asking for it.

Jeremiah said, let him that glories glory in this, that he understands and knows Me, that I am the Lord (Jer. 9:24). If we are to boast about anything, we should boast that we know the Lord. We cannot boast in our wisdom, might, or riches. It is God who gives us these things, and we need to give Him the glory for it. The false gods of this world are not able to give us anything so we can know them. As a matter of fact, the gods of this world are made according to what men and women want them to be. The first thing Paul prays for them is that they would grow in their knowledge of God. Paul says, may God give you spirit of wisdom in the knowledge of God. This is so we can know completely the wisdom of God. And may God give you spirit of revelation in the knowledge of God. This is to know complete revelation of who God is. Peter tells us to grow in the grace and knowledge of our Lord Jesus Christ (2 Pet. 3:18).

The second thing Paul prays for them is for "the eyes of your understanding being enlightened; that ye may know what is the hope of His calling" (Eph. 1:18). Some translations have it reading "the eyes of your heart" instead of "the eyes of your understanding." The *eyes of the heart* is a Jewish term, something Paul knows very well. *Enlightened* is to illuminate, that is, to understand. When the eyes of their hearts are enlightened, they can know the things of God. This adds to their spiritual growth. The more you know about God, the more you want to know about Him. May God give them the spirit of wisdom and revelation in the knowledge of God.

This is called spiritual understanding. It is like when the light bulb comes on, and they say, "Oh, now I get it." This is different from having an open mind. Having an open mind means being open to accept any teaching that is out there. This is different from the age of enlightenment, which taught to set people free from doctrines that had been around for thousands of years. This led people to doubt the Word of God. Paul prays that their hearts will be enlightened so that they will know the hope of His calling. A psalmist wrote, "Open Thou mine eyes, that I may behold wondrous things out of Thy Law" (Ps. 119:18). The psalmist's prayer is for God to reveal to him the wonderful things in God's Word. We need God to open the eyes of our minds so that we can understand His Word. There are wonderful things in His Word.

In terms of having the mind enlightened, or illuminated, so that they can know the hope of His calling, to know is to have knowledge of something. Hope is the confident expectation of something. Hope is not something wished for or desired. When most people use the word *hope*, they are unsure that it will happen. But Paul says to have the eyes enlightened is to know the confident expectation of His calling. Paul is saying that they will know the confident expectation of God's calling—His calling of them to salvation. They can know for certain of their salvation. It is not a hope; it is a confident expectation that they are saved.

It is God who does the calling. Paul wrote to the Romans, "moreover whom He did predestinate, them He also called: and whom He called, them He also justified: and whom He justified, them He also glorified" (Rom. 8:30). It is God calling men to salvation. It is the confident expectation of salvation. Whom God calls, He justifies, and so on. It is confident expectation that what God has started He will finish. He began with salvation, and it ends with glorification. It is God's calling, not man's. Paul said we are saved by hope (Rom. 8:24), which is the confident expectation of our salvation. Paul also said that God called us into His kingdom and glory (1 Thess. 2:12).

The third thing Paul prays for is that they would know "what the riches of the glory of His inheritance in the saints" (Eph. 1:18). This inheritance is different than the one mentioned in verse 11. That one referred to receiving or obtaining something. This one refers to receiving a possession as one's own. Paul said it is God's inheritance, not ours. Just like God's calling is His, not ours. We are God's glorious inheritance. Paul is praying that they will know who they are in Christ. Just as gold brings glory to the rich man, so the saints bring glory to God. It's not that they are rich with material things but that they are God's possession. They became God's inheritance because the blood of Christ purchased them. One day He will receive them and us as His inheritance.

Paul said "the saints," meaning holy ones or the ones set apart, are His inheritance. God set us apart for Him. We were separated from sin and set apart to God. Because of Jesus Christ, we are God's glorious inheritance. The riches of the glory of His inheritance in the saints could be read as the exceeding rich glory of His inheritance in the saints. We need to see what we are to God. We also need to have our eyes enlightened so that we can know the riches of the glory of His inheritance in the saints.

The fourth thing Paul prays that they would know is "what is the exceeding greatness of His power to us-ward us who believe according to the working of His might power" (Eph. 1:19). Paul is praying that their eyes will be enlightened so that they will have knowledge of God's power. God's power is exceeding, which means beyond or surpassing greatness. God's power is inseparable from Him. We can know God's power by reading the creation account in Genesis chapter 1. God created the heavens and the earth out of nothing. We can know God's power by reading of what He did to the Egyptians, delivering the Israelites, and parting the Red Sea (Exod. 12–14). We can know God's power by reading of the birth of the church in Acts chapter 2.

God's power is toward those who believe or, that is, one believing. Believers are the ones who put their trust in Christ, those who believe that He is Lord and Savior. They are the saints and the faithful, as

Paul mentioned in Ephesians 1:1. They believed in Jesus Christ and are sealed with the Holy Spirit (Eph. 1:13). They believe in Jesus when they heard the word of truth, which is the gospel of their salvation. The power of God is toward us in that we are His workmanship created in Christ Jesus (Eph. 2:10); that means we are His making, His product, created—that is, formed—in Christ Jesus. This does not refer to when God first created man. This is when God took a person and made him into a new creature, a new man in Christ. His power is toward us who believe that He begat us with the word of truth (James 1:18). The power of God is demonstrated in the gospel (Rom. 1:16), for it brings man to salvation through Christ.

His power is "according to the working of His mighty power" (Eph. 1:19). That is, in line with His operating power exercised by His strength. It means God's surpassingly powerful power that is in line with the operation of the strength of His might. It is His might that He exercises to those who believe and those who will believe. It is only God who can take a person and make him or her into a new creature. His power to do that is according to the operating of His strength. God exercises His strength through those of us who believe. To truly become a new person is through strength of God. To turn over a new leaf or go through a program is to do so in a person's own strength. God's power produces effects. It is God's power that changes our vile bodies (Phil. 3:21). It is the word of His power that is upholding all things (Heb. 1:3). All things are being maintained by His word. Peter said we are kept by the power of God through faith (1 Pet. 1:5). This means military guarded. It does not mean you live your life as you please and God will protect you, but that through faith in Christ, those who are believers, God will protect, meaning they won't lose their salvation.

"Which He wrought in Christ, when He raised Him from the dead" (Eph. 1:20). The power that is toward us is the same power that raised Jesus from the dead. It is God's surpassingly powerful power, according to God's operating of His might. It is His power that is active and energetic in Christ. Of all things that God has exercised by His strength, nothing is as powerful as what He worked in Christ. No man can have this power. The power that is toward believers is seen in the resurrection of Christ. Christ was raised for our justification. We wouldn't have salvation if not for the resurrection of Christ. Our faith and our hope would be useless if God did not have the power to raise Jesus from the dead.

Paul said "and if Christ be not raised, your faith is vain; ye are yet in your sins. Then they also which are fallen asleep in Christ are perished. If in this life only we have hoped in Christ, we are of all men most miserable" (1 Cor. 15:17–19). If God did not have the power to raise Christ from the dead, we are not saved; we are still in our sins. If God did not have the power to raise Christ from the dead, then those who have died in hope are to remain in the grave. If we have nothing to look forward to, we are most miserable. But that is not the case. God's surpassing greatness of power is active and energetic in Christ. His power did not die when Christ died. His power was still active and energetic, waiting to be displayed three days later.

Peter preached this message on the day of Pentecost. He spoke of God raising Christ from the dead and placing Him and His right hand (Acts 2:24–33). David wrote in Psalms, speaking of Christ not staying in the grave long enough to see decay, speaking of Jesus's resurrection (Ps. 16:10). Not only is God's surpassing greatness of power according to the strength of His might, active in the resurrection, but it also in Him seating Jesus at His right hand. "And set Him at His own right hand in the heavenly places" (Eph. 1:20). The right hand is the place of authority and power. David also wrote of Jesus's seating at the right hand of God in Psalms 110:1. Jesus said to the high priest at His trial that he would see the Son of Man sitting at the right hand of power (Matt. 26:64). Stephen, while he was being martyred, saw Jesus sitting at the right hand of God (Acts 7:56).

His place is in the heavenly places. That is in heaven, His place of authority and power that no man can threaten to take away. By the power of God, Christ is exalted to His right hand and has been given authority and power by God Himself. God's power is toward us through salvation, but His surpassing greatness of power toward us is working in Christ.

"Far above all principality, and power, and might, and dominion, and every name that is named" (Eph.1:21). His place in the heavenly places is greatly higher than (1) all principality, which is rule or government, the one granting power; (2) all power, which is authority, meaning someone with official power who has the authority to do; (3) all might, meaning all power, which is a sovereign or king; (4) all dominion, meaning all rulers or lordships; and (5) all or every name, which means an authority or dignity who is assigned a name or a title. Whether it is a president, lord chancellor, king, or queen, Christ is greatly higher. Christ is above anybody who is in the place of power and authority. No matter who is in power, whether here in the United States or in another county, Christ is greatly higher than them. A ruler could rule the world, yet Christ will still be greatly higher than that person. God has given Jesus Christ that power and authority above all others.

"God has highly exalted Christ, and given Him a name which is above every name: that at the name of Jesus every knee should bow, of things in heaven, and things in earth, and things under the earth" (Phil. 2:9–10). Notice that Paul likes to use the word *and*. This is typical for him. Here he uses it to show that Jesus is higher than all of these things. One is not above the other, but Christ is above them all. God has raised Jesus to the highest position, to supreme majesty. God has raised no one higher than Jesus Christ. His name is above every name, and at the name of Jesus, every knee shall bow. Every knee includes everything in heaven, which is the angels and the departed saints; all things on earth, including kings and common people, good and bad people; and all things under the earth, which is the devil, his demons, and the dead. That's the power of Jesus's name. In the name of Jesus we baptize (Matt. 28:19), and in the name of Jesus there is salvation (Acts 4:12). There is not another name in which we baptize, and there is no other name that can give us salvation.

"Not only in this world, but also in that which is to come" (Eph. 1:21). Jesus is greatly higher than anyone and anything in this age and the age that is about to come. In other words, Jesus Christ is greatly higher than all who are in the place of authority and power right now. In Paul's time, there were tyrant emperors who didn't mind killing. But Christ was over them in that time. This brought comfort to martyrs. As they faced their killers, verses that say that Jesus above any name brought them comfort. Just knowing that Christ was above all others meant that one day they would bow down at the name of Jesus.

Not only is Jesus above all the rulers of nations, but He is also over the angelic beings. Principalities, powers, and rulers of the darkness are referred to as evil angelic beings. Paul says that we wrestle against them and not flesh and blood (Eph. 6:12). The evil spirits are subject to Jesus, and the proof of this is found in the gospels. The devil is subject to Jesus (Rev. 20:10). Jesus is greatly higher in the age to come. This is the heavenly kingdom. This is for all eternity.

"And hath put all things under His feet" (Eph. 1:22). With Jesus Christ being exalted above all things, sitting at the right hand of God, He has put all things in subjection. Under His feet, express subjection. All things are subject to Christ. All things not only include what we just read as far as principalities, powers, might, and dominion but creation as well. Man was originally to have dominion over the animals, but man failed to do this when Adam and Eve sinned in the garden. Put all things under His feet is a prophecy from Psalms 8:6–8: "Thou madest Him to have dominion over the works of Thy hands; Thou hast put all things under His feet: all sheep and oxen, yea, and the beasts of the field; the fowl of the air, and the fish of the sea, and whatsoever passeth through the paths of the seas." All the works of God Christ is over; everything is subject to Him. Jesus said, "All power is given to Me in heaven and in earth" (Matt. 28:18). All authority is given to Jesus Christ in heaven and on the earth. With all things under the feet of Jesus, that means He is over all things.

"And gave Him to be the head over all things to the church, which is the body, the fulness of Him that filleth all in all" (Eph. 1:22–23). God gave Jesus to be the head of the church. That means that God gave Jesus to be the Lord, or the authority, over the church. Along with everything else under the feet of Jesus, God gave Him the church, of which He is the head, or the authority. We are not talking about the building but rather the believers. Believers in Christ are the church. It is the saved, not people, who are on the rolls of the churches. Just because someone goes to church and is the member of the church does not mean that he or she is the church. Those who have put their trust in Jesus Christ as Lord and Savior are the church.

The church was born on Pentecost (Acts 2). Jesus is the Lord of the church, meaning He has the authority to judge them (Rev. 2–3). Jesus

23

already said it is His church (Matt. 16:18). The church is His body. The fullness of Him is that which complements or completes. Filleth all in all means to fill, to make full, or to fill to fullness. Jesus supplies the church with everything it needs.

Ephesians Chapter 2

Chapter 2 of Ephesians covers the past and present condition. Salvation by grace through faith is discussed in verses 1–10 and peace and unity through Christ in verses 11–22.

"And you hath He quickened, who were dead in trespasses and sins" (Eph. 2:1). This verse could be read, "and you being dead in your trespasses and sins," or it could be read as, "you when you were dead in trespasses and sins." Paul is not pointing a finger at the Ephesians or accusing them of sins. He is reminding them of their past condition. He reminds them that they were once dead without Christ and that the power of God made them alive in Christ. The power of God toward the believer is that they have been made alive. Who can take a dead man and make him alive? Jesus said He came to give life (John 10:10). Jesus said He is the resurrection and the life and that any man who believes in Him will not die (John 11:25–26). God can, and He demonstrated His power by doing so. Paul is saying you who He has made alive who were once dead. Paul wrote to the Colossians, "and you, being dead in your sins and the uncircumcision of your flesh, hath He quickened together with Him, having forgiven you all trespasses" (Col. 2:13). God can take a person dead in his or her trespasses and sins and make him or her alive.

Dead means spiritually dead. It refers to the condition of the person without Christ. It is without hope of eternal life. Being dead spiritually is the result of sin in the garden. God told Adam that he could eat of any tree in the garden except for the tree of knowledge of good and evil. If he did, he and Eve would die (Gen. 2:16–17). Physical death came into the world because they ate from this tree. It's not that the tree was poisonous, but to eat from it gave them the knowledge of good and evil.

To do good is to obey the command of God, and to do evil is to disobey. Since Adam disobeyed the command of God, he then knew good and evil.

The father of the prodigal son said that his son was dead and now is alive (Luke 15:24). This means that when the son was living in sin, he was dead, but since he repented and came back to the father, he was considered alive. To be dead spiritually is to be dead to God. You have no spiritual life within you. If a person remains in his or her sins and trespasses, that person will be dead, even though he or she is physically living.

Paul says the Ephesians were dead in their trespasses, meaning they had fallen aside. To trespass is to purposefully step over boundary or rule. It is considered to fall aside or a sideslip. It is falling from a known path, actively breaking the rule. It is the same word as *sin* in Ephesians 1:7. But the word *sins* in Ephesians 2:1 means to miss the mark, to give offense to God. It is missing the true goal. Paul is reminding them that they were once like this. They were missing the true mark and actively breaking the rule, or overstepping a known boundary, which was an offense to God. This speaks of the depth of our sins. When we were without Christ dead in our sins, we were deliberately stepping over and missing the true mark that God had established.

Certain things in men's conscience are wrong. One example is murder. Since we were dead in our trespasses and sins, we purposely stepped over these boundaries and missed the mark God had set; thus, we became an offense to God. Being dead in our trespasses and sins means that the quickening life-giving Spirit has not given us life. Dead in trespasses and sins is the description of the natural and unregenerate person. That person is without life. This leads to the second death.

"Wherein in time past ye walked according to the course of this world" (Eph. 2:2). In this verse, Paul is saying that at one time you lived in line with the age of the world, an evil age. At some time in the past, the Ephesians were dead in trespasses and sins, and being dead, they lived according to the age. That is, they lived according to the world system, a life apart from Christ. It was a life full of sin. Paul gave examples of how people lived according to that evil age. These are found in 1 Corinthians 6:9–10 and Titus 3:3. Peter also provided examples of how people lived in line with the evil age, and they are found in 1 Peter 4:3. John wrote that the whole world lies in wickedness (1 John 5:19). The Ephesians and others of that time used to live their lives in this way, and people continue to live this way today.

"According to the prince of the power of the air" (Eph. 2:2). Not only did the Ephesians live according to the evil age, but they also lived according to the prince of the power of the air. That is Satan. The power of the air is the region of demons, spiritual rulers, and demonic angels. Satan is the ruler of the air, so he is the ruler of the present evil age. When people live according to the evil age, they live according to Satan's rule. He is deceiving them. This does not mean that people can blame Satan for their wrongdoing. He does not have that kind of power. He deceives people into doing what he wants them to do, but the choice is within the power of the person who does the work. They live according to his rule.

Many deny Satan's existence, but Scripture shows that he exists and is active and present. When Adam and Eve were in the Garden of Eden, Satan deceived Eve into eating from the tree of knowledge of good and evil (Gen. 3:1–7). You can read the first two chapters of Job and see how Satan worked (Job 1:6–2:8). In the temptations of Jesus, Satan tried to get Jesus to fall (Matt. 4:1–11; Mark 1:12–13; Luke 4:1–13). Satan's demons were working too, as they possessed people and tormented them. Satan will be locked up in the bottomless pit for a thousand years (Rev. 20:1–3). He doesn't have the power that God has, and we have already read in Ephesians chapter 1 that Satan and his demons are subject to Jesus Christ.

Since Satan cannot occupy more than one place at a time, he has his demons do his work. Paul says that we wrestle against spiritual wickedness in high places (Eph. 6:12), which means that we are not fighting against man but against Satan and his demons. When people are dead in trespasses and sins, they live according to Satan and his rule. Ephesians 2:2 continues: "the spirit that now worketh in the children of disobedience." Again, this is referencing Satan and his demons. This spirit is presently active and effective in rebellious sons. When people live lives of sin, they are under the control Satan. This is not to say that they are possessed by demons, but they are under Satan's influence. We can say that this evil spirit is very effective in the way things are going today, in modern times.

This spirit was effective in Judas as he betrayed Jesus (Luke 22:2–3; John 13:2). This spirit was active in Ananias and Sapphira as they plotted to lie to the Holy Spirit (Acts 5). Paul said that the god of this world has blinded the minds of them who believe not (2 Cor. 4:4). The apostle John wrote that he who commits sin is of the devil (1 John 3:8). He is saying that a person who habitually sins is of the devil. We can see this same spirit active today as men become increasingly wicked.

Paul says the spirit is active and effective in the sons of disobedience. They are rebellious, which means they do not live according to God's rules. They reject Christ, remove His Word from public places, and try to separate Christianity from people's lives. Isaiah said woe to the rebellious children for they do not take counsel from God (Isa. 30:1). They take advice, but it's not from God. They have rejected His Word. Jesus told the Jews, "Ye are children of your father the devil, and the lusts of your father ye will do" (John 8:44). The children of rebellion will live according to the evil age and according to the devil. The devil will use anybody he can to fulfill his desires.

"Among whom also we all had our conversation in time past in the lusts of our flesh, fulfilling the desires of the flesh and of the mind" (Eph. 2:3). In this passage, Paul switches from the second person singular (you, your) to first person plural (we, our). You were made alive in Ephesians 2:1, and you walked according to the course of this world in Ephesians 2:2. The Ephesians were Gentiles; they were to whom Paul was referring in verses 1 and 2; now in verse 3, he includes the Jews, which includes himself, for he says "we also" and "of our flesh." Isaiah included himself when prophesying (Isa. 53:5, 64:6–7), and Daniel did the same (Dan. 9:5–9). When Ezra and Nehemiah prayed, they included themselves in their prayers (Ezra 9:5–15; Neh. 1:5–11). So it's common for godly men to include themselves when they confess sins of the nation or when preaching to others. When Paul wrote to Titus, he included himself when he listed the sins of ungodly people (Titus 3:3). Even Peter did the same (1 Pet. 4:3).

The word *conversation* does not mean talk. It is live. So Paul is saying that we lived among the sons of disobedience; we were once rebellious to God. Paul has said in times past that we lived in the lusts of the flesh. We have fulfilled the desires of the flesh and of the mind. So, once upon a time we lived like the sons of disobedience. The Jews, including Paul, were no different than the Gentiles.

Lust is a longing, to set the heart upon or to desire something. Lust has been included with three other human emotions: fear, pleasure, and grief. All four are harmful to a person's moral thinking. Basically, these four emotions have been taught and keep us from thinking straight. Once fear is in a person's heart, he or she cannot move. The same goes for pleasure and grief; once these things grip a person, he or she cannot think rationally. Once lust enters a person's heart, rational thinking leaves. That person does not act straight when lust has taken control. James wrote that when lust is conceived, it brings forth sin, and sin, when it is finished, brings forth death (James 1:15).

It has also been thought that the sinful motivation of the heart is just as bad as the sinful act itself. That is, if someone has an evil desire within his or her mind, it is just as bad as if he or she were acting upon it. What is in the heart usually comes out. Jesus said if you lust after a woman in your heart, you have already committed adultery (Matt. 5:28), and that's without acting upon it.

Lust is impulsive and includes sensual desires. It is the natural tendency toward evil things. Paul is not talking about desires for good things like peace or food. He is talking about evil desires, a longing for what is not permissible for believers. Flesh means human nature and is not referring to the skin. So at some point the Ephesians were in the desires of their human nature.

Paul says they were also fulfilling, that is carrying out, the will of the human nature and of the thoughts. At some point we have all experienced the will, inclination, or desire of our human nature and of the mind. Flesh is human nature; it is natural to do things contrary to the Word of God. People can be moral, but there is a tendency toward sin. Paul said in Romans 8:8 that those who are in the flesh cannot please God. No matter how moral a person is, without Christ, he or she is still in the flesh, fulfilling his or her desires, and cannot please God. Paul put the Jews and Gentiles in one boat. Everybody is the same. Everybody before Christ at some point has lived in the lusts of the flesh, carrying out the desires of the flesh and of the mind. People who are without Christ continue to live that way. Paul reminds us that all have sinned and fallen short of the glory of God (Rom. 3:23). Paul gave us a list of the works of the flesh in Galatians 5:19–21.

Peter told us to "abstain from fleshly lusts, which war against the soul" (1 Pet. 2:11). We need to refrain from lust, which wars against the soul; that is, we need to keep from acting upon it. Lustful thoughts need to be condemned just as much as acting upon them. The apostle John wrote, "for all that is in the world, the lust of the flesh, and the lust of the eyes, and the pride of life, is not of the Father, but is of the world" (1 John 2:16). With these three things, Satan tempted Eve in the garden (Gen. 3:1–6). Satan also tempted Jesus with these same three things (Matt. 4:1–11). The lust of the flesh is to desire something that satisfies the appetites; the lust of the eyes means desiring something that looks good; and the pride of life is the same as arrogant boasting.

Paul says, "and were by nature the children of wrath, even as others" (Eph. 2:3). Nature is a native disposition. A person who is born of a certain country or city would be inclined to live with the customs in which they grew up. It is the way they know, and so they continue to live in according to those customs. It is natural for them to live that way, though others may think it is strange. If you were born and raised in the South, you would live according to the customs of the South, and so it goes if you were born in another part of the country. Paul is saying that by nature we live according to our customs, which in this case is sin.

The word *children* describes the connection by birth. So, by birth we are children of wrath. Wrath is anger, which implies judgment, and it has the view of revenge. Wrath means more than lasing in nature; in other words, it does not mean losing one's temper but rather displaying the anger. When someone looses his or her temper, it usually flares up and then dies. The type of anger Paul is referring to is displayed through revenge and punishment. We are sons of wrath because we live in the flesh and have committed the will of the flesh and mind. This is not saying that little children deserve God's wrath because they have been born into sin. But it does say that because they grow up in and live in the flesh (i.e., commit the desires of the flesh), they continue to live in the flesh and therefore have the wrath of God upon them.

Children don't know any better, but they need to be taught. By nature, we are born to have God's punishment on us. Why? Because we are sinful people. David wrote, "Behold I was shapen in iniquity, and in sin did my mother conceive me" (Ps. 51:5). This was after David's affair with Bathsheba, which we can read in 2 Samuel chapters 11 and 12. In other words, David is saying that he was brought forth in wickedness, or sin, and that in sin, which is to miss the way or goal, his mother conceived him. This is not saying that his mother had an adulterous relationship but that because she by nature is a sinner, so was David. David is saying that by nature, man's tendency is to sin. This is one trait we receive from both parents. This goes on from generation to generation.

In Psalm 58:3, it is written, "The wicked are estranged from the womb: they go astray as soon as they be born, speaking lies." From birth, they go astray. From day one, people are sinners. If you think about it, you don't have to teach a child to lie. It's there by nature, and we cannot escape from it. No matter what a person does, he or she is by nature a sinner. It is in the attitudes and motives of people. We cannot use this as an excuse to sin. At some point, we all have been children of wrath and we all have been deserving of God's punishment. Paul is referring to the time before Christ, before salvation. Paul has put both Jew and Gentile into one category, and all are under sin (Rom. 3:9) and again all have sinned and fallen short of God's glory (Rom. 3:23). Paul says even others—meaning the Jews—lived the same way as the Gentiles. Paul goes on to explain how they are no longer children of wrath in the next few verses.

"But God, who is rich in mercy, for His great love wherewith He loved us" (Eph. 2:4). God has abounding compassion because of the great love with which He loved us. Even though we were born as children of wrath, God loved us and had compassion for us. Paul wrote to the Romans, "but God who commendeth His love toward us, in that, while we were yet sinners, Christ died for us" (Rom. 5:8). God showed His love through Christ dying for us. If God did not love us, He wouldn't have had compassion on us, and if He didn't have compassion on us, we would still be the children of wrath and deserving of punishment. God is not a god who is not concerned with people. He saw our need and moved to meet it. Our need was a savior, and that savior is Jesus Christ. We needed redeeming and forgiveness. This was granted through the death of Christ.

"Herein is love, not that we loved God, but that He loved us, and sent His Son to be the propitiation for our sins" (1 John 4:10). God loved us and sent Jesus, His Son, to be the atonement for our sins. So many people judge God's love by how their lives are going. Some people say that if God loved them this and that would not have happened. But God's love is not based on circumstances. Malachi dealt with this during his ministry (Mal. 1:2). Basically, God said He loved them, but they questioned His love. God said He loved them because He chose them.

God had compassion on us, and He demonstrated His love toward us through Jesus Christ. His love was such that He turned His back on Jesus when He was on the cross. That's why Jesus cried out, "My God, My God, why hast Thou forsaken Me" (Matt. 27:46). Just as the Old Testament priests had to offer sacrifices for the atonement of sin, Christ is our atonement. There is no longer a need to offer bulls or goats since Jesus died on the cross. He loved us even though we were children of wrath and sinful people. Because of God's great love for us, He had compassion on us, and since He had compassion on us, we now have salvation.

Paul now moves on to God's work in us: "Even when we were dead in sins" (Eph. 2:5). This part of the verse is referring to when we, speaking of the Jews, were dead in sins. Just as the Gentiles were dead in their sins, so were the Jews. He "hath quickened us together with Christ, (by grace ye are saved)" (Eph. 2:5). God has made the Jews alive together with the Gentiles with Christ. They have a new life, just as the Gentiles do, and that new life is in Christ. Paul says, "By grace ye are saved," which in Greek literally means "by whose grace you are saved." It is by the grace of God that the Gentiles have been saved. It is God's favor upon the Gentiles that they are saved. God could have left the Gentiles in their sins, but He has love and compassion for them, just as He did for the Jews.

"And hath raised us up together" (Eph. 2:6). This means to arouse from death, and both the Jews and Gentiles have been aroused from death together. Just as Jesus Christ was physically raised from the dead, the Jew and Gentile believers are spiritually raised from the dead. When we were dead in our sins, we had no spiritual life in us. Just as a dead person is lifeless, so it is with a spiritually dead person: the Holy Spirit is not living within them. Even though the person is physically living, that person is spiritually dead. Paul is saying here that we who were once dead in our sins have been resurrected to a new life in Christ. When people are baptized, it is a symbol that they have been given new life. We can read about this in Romans 6:4–5; Colossians 2:12–13; and Colossians 3:1–3.

"And made us sit together in heavenly places in Christ Jesus" (Eph. 2:6). This means that both Jews and Gentiles will sit down together in heaven. One day in heaven we will be seated with Jesus Christ. "That in the ages to come he might shew the exceeding riches of his grace in his kindness toward us through Christ Jesus" (Eph. 2:7). "In the ages to come" means when the times arrives, referring to Christ's return, and for all eternity will God display the surpassing riches of His grace in His kindness toward us. Notice the word *together.* Paul is saying *us,* the Jews along with the Ephesians (the Gentiles). Together, the Jewish and Gentile believers have been given new life; together they have been raised; together they will sit in the heavenly places. This is through Jesus Christ and Him alone.

"For by grace are ye saved through faith; and that not of yourselves: it is the gift of God" (Eph. 2:8). Remember, grace is undeserved favor. It is by God's undeserved favor that we are saved. Remember also that we were children of wrath, living according to Satan's rule, living in sin, and dead in our sin. So salvation is by grace, if not who would be saved. Knowing who we were, who would have saved us and who would have shown grace to us? Who has compassion on people like those Paul mentioned in the previous verses? Those who believe in Christ immediately receive salvation. Paul is reminding them that salvation is by God's grace. Salvation does not happen without His grace. If not for God's grace, salvation wouldn't be by grace. Also, we cannot be saved without believing. Grace is God's part, and believing is ours.

"Salvation not of yourselves" means it's not something man came up with. In other words, salvation is not an invention of man. If it were something manmade, would there be any need for salvation? If it were something manmade, to whom would it be offered? Since we are the children of wrath, who would receive salvation? If man invented salvation, would it be offered by grace? No. There would be favoritism. And if it were manmade, would it be a gift? God offered salvation as a gift to man, and a gift is free for the person to whom it is offered, but the person offering the gift had to pay for it. It was God who paid for our salvation so that we could have it for free.

"Not of works, lest any man should boast" (Eph. 2:9). Not only is salvation not manmade, but it is not of works. To work for salvation means to seek justification by doing good works. The reason salvation is not of works is so no one can boast about it. If salvation is by works, then many people are saved. Anybody can be saved through doing good works. Paul says salvation is not of works so that no one may boast of what they have done. Paul also said if anybody had any right to boast about what they have done, it would be Abraham, but not before God (Rom. 4:2). But again, if anybody had any right to boast or glory, wouldn't it be Paul? To boast is to be prideful for what you have done. To take pride in salvation by works is like saying, "I have done such and such, and it is good enough to be saved." If that is the way to salvation, they would spread the news about it, and others would do the same.

Paul said to the Romans, "Now to him that worketh is the reward not reckoned of grace, but of debt. But to him that worketh not, but believeth on Him that justifieth the ungodly, his faith is counted for righteousness" (Rom. 4:4–5). The one who is working is trying to earn something; his payment is not of favor but of something owed. Basically, it is an expectation to receive something for work done. So, if a person works for salvation, he expects to receive salvation. That's what the false religions want you to do. One of them teaches that you must do such and such to be included in the number of people in heaven. If you try to work for your salvation, the whole time you are hoping that you have done enough to receive it. Some teach that you must do good to outweigh the bad. Again, you hope you have done enough. Who's to say if what is enough? It would be terrible if you had done all you could and it wasn't enough. Paul is saying that for he who works for salvation, it is not of grace but of debt.

On the other hand, to he who is working not for salvation but believes in God who justifies, his faith is counted for righteousness. Paul is not saying that a Christian should not work, but his or her work should be out of love for the Lord and not required for salvation. That person does not believe his or her works save him or her. Rather, that person knows that he or she is saved because he or she believed in God who justifies and as a result he or she works or demonstrates that he or she is saved. If we must work for salvation, it is not a gift and it is not of grace, and it becomes drudgery. If we must work for salvation, who sets the standard and who determines what work saves and what work doesn't? If salvation were by works, there would be many ways to be saved. How can salvation be a gift if you must work for it? Paul said he who glories, let him glory in the Lord (1 Cor. 1:31). That means if anybody should boast, let him boast in the Lord. Salvation is from God, not of man.

"For we are His workmanship" (Eph. 2:10). The reason we cannot boast in our salvation is that we are God's workmanship. That is, we are something that is made, handiwork. "Created in Christ Jesus unto good works" (Eph. 2:10). This means we were created in Christ Jesus for good works. We are made by God, created in Christ Jesus, unto good works. The verse continues: "which God hath before ordained that we should walk in them" (Eph. 2:10). God has prepared beforehand that we should live in good works. God has prepared beforehand that we should not work for salvation, but to be His handiwork, created in Christ Jesus unto good works.

"Wherefore remember, that ye being in time past Gentiles in the flesh, who are called Uncircumcision by that which is called the Circumcision in the flesh made by hands" (Eph. 2:11). Paul is telling the Ephesian believers to remember who they were. They are to call to mind their former state, meaning what they were in the past, Gentiles in the flesh. Gentiles are non-Jews, which implies that they were heathens or pagans. The Gentiles were known to worship false idols (1 Cor. 12:2). The Jewish term *Gentile* is one of hate and scorn. Gentiles were considered unclean, and it was unlawful for Jews to be friends with them. The disciples were told not to go to the Gentiles but only to the house of Israel (Matt. 10:5). Jesus also said that salvation is of the Jews (John 4:22). The Gentiles were considered enemies of God; they were not allowed to have knowledge of

God, they were not allowed to be counseled by the Jews, and children born of mixed marriages were considered illegitimate.

Paul is saying that they were once Gentiles in the flesh, who were called Uncircumcision. In other words, the Jews used the term *uncircumcision* as an insult. The Jews were the Circumcision in the flesh, indicating that they were in the covenant with God. The book of Genesis gives us the covenant of circumcision (17:10–14), and it was between Abraham and God. To be circumcised is to be part of the covenant family. Notice what Paul has to say about the circumcision: in the flesh made by hands. This means that they were physically circumcised and it was an outward symbol. The circumcision caused trouble for Gentile believers (Acts 15:1; Gal. 6:12).

Basically, the Jews were saying that you couldn't be saved unless you are circumcised and you cannot be part of the covenant family unless you go through the ritual of circumcision. True circumcision is not physical but spiritual. Uncircumcision refers to those who still live in sin. So it doesn't matter if someone has been circumcised or not because it never indicated that the circumcised man was a man of faith, and Paul dealt with this in Romans 2:26–29. The Jews had a holier-than-thou type of attitude that God never intended. It continues to this day.

"That at that time ye were without Christ, being aliens from the commonwealth of Israel, and strangers from the covenants of promise, having no hope, and without God in the world" (Eph. 2:12). "At that time" refers to during the time that the Ephesian believers were Gentiles in the flesh. Being Gentiles in the flesh here means they weren't believers.

As Gentiles in the flesh, that is being uncircumcised, they were strangers from the community of Israel. This means that they were excluded from the commonwealth of Israel; they were shut out of the fellowship with Israel. They were not part of the nation of Israel. The Jews were God's chosen people, so they had certain rights and privileges. The term *alien* is used today to refer to those who come into this land. Because they are such, they do not have the rights and privileges that citizens have. Because Gentiles are not part of the covenant family, they are excluded from everything pertaining to the Jews.

Paul continues by saying they were strangers or foreigners to the covenants of the promise. Notice that Paul did not say they were strangers or aliens to these things as if they were new to them; he said it as if they had no part in it. God never made a covenant with the Gentiles. The Gentiles can never claim what God promised Israel. This promise was made to Abraham, Isaac, and Jacob. The word *covenants* refer to more than one, but there is one promise, *the* promise, and it was the promise of the Messiah, Jesus Christ. The covenant was with Israel, and His promise was for Israel. A covenant is a contract; it is an agreement and a promise that is legally binding. The covenant that God made, he will never break (Judg. 2:1).

They had no hope. In other words, there was nothing for them. The Gentiles were in a hopeless situation. This hope is not like the hope of getting what you want for Christmas. This hope means to have a confident expectation of receiving something or knowing for sure that you will receive something. Because they were in times past, Gentiles in the flesh, they had no confident expectation of anything that pertained to the Jews. With promises made only to Israel, what could they expect?

They are without God in the world. They are godless, atheists. They did not have knowledge of God, and as a result they were immoral, excluded from communion with God and from the privileges given to Israel. They had some knowledge of God, but they lived their lives as if He didn't exist. Paul talked about this in Romans (1:19–28). The Gentiles had many gods but were without the true God. When Paul was in Athens, he saw the city given up to worshipping gods (Acts 17:16–23). Paul said to the Galatians, "howbeit then, when ye knew not God, ye did service unto them which by nature are no gods" (Gal. 4:8). When they did not know God, they were worshipping gods. And as Paul put it, they are no gods. He also said they were demons (1 Cor. 10:20).

That is what it is like to be Gentile in the flesh. The Jews used that against them. But Paul said, "But now in Christ Jesus ye who sometimes were far off are made nigh by the blood of Christ" (Eph. 2:13). There was hostility between the Jews and the Gentiles. In verse 12, Paul told the Gentiles to remember who they were before Christ. Now, in Christ they are no longer what they were. Their time as Gentiles is the past, and Paul is bringing them to the present. This verse could be read to mean the same thing today, in modern times: in Christ Jesus you being once at a distance are brought near by the blood of Christ. This means that the Gentiles are no longer far away. They are now brought near by the blood of Christ. The Jews used their position against the Gentiles, and now Paul is saying that is no longer the case in Christ.

"For He is our peace, who hath made both one, and hath broken down the middle wall of partition between us" (Eph. 2:14). Jesus is the peace between the Jew and the Gentile. During a peace talk between two nations, there is usually a compromise. But here there are no compromises. One group did not have to do something to have peace, and the other did not have to stop something to have peace. There was no shaking of hands, signing a contract, or any other action to promise that each party would keep its end of the contract. Through Jesus Christ there is peace between Jews and Gentiles. Jesus is the one who made both one. There are no longer Jews and Gentiles when it comes to salvation. The Gentile has been brought near through Jesus Christ. This means that Jews and Gentiles have the same promise when it comes to salvation. One group does not have an advantage over the other. Through the blood of Jesus, there is peace between both groups, they are both one.

Peter said it was against the law for the Jews to keep company with the Gentiles (Acts 10:28). Peter also contended with the Jews about going to the Gentiles when he called to go (Acts 11:2–3). Jesus spoke to the woman at the well, and she reminded Him that the Jews had no dealings with Samaritans (John 4:9) because the Samaritans were a mixed people of Jew and Gentile. The disciples were amazed that Jesus spoke to her (John 4:27).

Jesus destroyed the wall separating the Jew and Gentile. Paul said, "Where there is neither Greek nor Jew, circumcision nor uncircumcision, Barbarian, Scythian, bond nor free, but Christ is all, and in all" (Col. 3:11). *Barbarian* is non-Greek, referring to the Romans. When the Romans took over, they applied the same term to those who did not speak the same language or have the same customs as them. *Scythian* is a wild barbarian, someone who is more barbaric than the barbarian. Even here you can see the hostility between groups. Christ is all for all men, no matter who they are. Christ destroyed that separating fence between Jew and Gentile and for other races as well.

"Having abolished in His flesh the enmity, even the law of

commandments contained in ordinances" (Eph. 2:15). To abolish is to make null and void, render entirely useless, put an end to, or reduce to inactivity. "In His flesh" references Jesus's body, and the enmity is the hostility. This means at the death of Christ, His body put an end to the hostility between the Jew and Gentile. Paul says even the law of commandments contained in ordinances has been put to an end. This means that certain laws that the Jews were supposed to follow did not apply anymore, including the ceremonial law, the dietary restrictions, and ritual cleanness. All were abolished in the body of Jesus. Only the moral law still applies today.

The law Paul is referring to is the Mosaic law that separated the Jew from the Gentile. Following these commandments, people could distinguish between the Jew and the Gentile. The law was the separating fence between them. Because of the death of Christ, the Jew can no longer use that against the Gentile. Now they have no reason to call the Gentiles uncircumcised. Paul already made it clear that those who live in sin are uncircumcised. But that doesn't give anybody the right to call unbelievers names.

"For to make in Himself of twain one new man, so making peace" (Eph. 2:15). Jesus Christ did this to make in Himself one new man of two. In other words, Jesus made one new man from two different groups. *New* means something unlike before. So, when they became one new man, it was something that could not have been before, and they are no longer Jew and Gentile. There's unity between the two groups in Christ, where naturally it would not be otherwise. If the wall were still there, the hostility would still be there. But in Christ all that has been destroyed, and the law that was the fence has been made of no effect. The purpose of Christ's death is to make two groups one and so make peace between them. When a man tries to do away with a barrier, he forces it. But when Christ destroys the barrier, it is gone.

"And that He might reconcile both unto God in one body by the cross, having slain the enmity thereby" (Eph. 2:16). That Jesus might fully reconcile, or change from one condition to another, was His purpose. His body on the cross was to fully reconcile the Jew and Gentile to God. To reconcile is to end the conflict. The hostility has been put to death by the death of Jesus on the cross. He offered His body to reconcile both groups unto God. When someone trusts Christ as their Lord and Savior, that person become one with other believers. Regardless of race, social status, or background, once that person believes in Christ, he or she becomes one with other believers.

"And came and preached peace to you which were afar off, and to them that were nigh" (Eph. 2:17). Jesus came and announced the good news, and this good news is of peace. The Gentiles are the ones who were at a distance. The Jews are the ones who were near. The good news is for everyone. When Christ was born, the angels announced peace on earth (Luke 2:14). Isaiah called Jesus the Prince of Peace and said peace shall have no end (Isa. 9:6–7). There is not one gospel for one race and a different gospel for another race; there is only one gospel, and it is the gospel of Jesus Christ. There is not one gospel for one nation and a different one for another nation; it is the same gospel of Jesus Christ. Not only is there peace with one another when we trust Jesus as our Lord and Savior, but we also have peace with God. Paul said, "therefore being justified by faith, we have peace with God through our Lord Jesus Christ" (Rom. 5:1).

"For through Him we both have access by one Spirit unto the Father" (Eph. 2:18). Through Jesus we both, referring to Jews and Gentiles, have access to God. Gentiles are the non-Jewish race, and the name refers to all races in the world. Through Jesus, everybody has access to God. But only through Jesus Christ. To have access is to be brought into the presence of or to be given admission or permission to approach. It is through Jesus Christ, and without Him we cannot have access to God. Jesus said, "I am the Way, the Truth, and the Life: no man cometh to the Father, but by Me" (John 14:6). Jesus is the way, meaning there is no other way to the Father. Not all paths lead to Him. "Jesus is the truth" means that what He says is not lies and what He says comes from the Father. "Jesus is the life" means in Him is life and that everlasting life comes from Him. Jesus also said that He is the door (John 10:7,9). So, if you want access to God, you must come through Jesus Christ.

The Jews cannot have access to the Father by following the law, and the Gentiles cannot have access to the Father by any other means they invent. We are brought into the presence of God by one Spirit, and that is the Holy Spirit. Since Jew and Gentile are one through Jesus, both have access to God by the same Spirit. By the Holy Spirit we have access to God, with acceptance. To "have admission to approach" means we can be brought into the presence of God.

During the time of the exodus, Moses was the only one who was allowed access to God (Exod. 24:2). For the Day of Atonement, only the high priest was allowed access to God (Lev. 16:12–15). Now through Jesus Christ, believers have access to God (Rom. 5:2). Through Jesus Christ the Gentile has access to God; through Jesus Christ the Jew has access to God; and both are brought into His presence by His Spirit. Now through Jesus Christ we can enter the holiest with boldness (Heb. 10:19). All believers have access to God and can approach Him by His Spirit.

"Now therefore ye are no more strangers and foreigners, but fellowcitizens with the saints, and of the household of God" (Eph. 2:19). Paul is referring to the Gentiles as no more strangers and foreigners. Remember, in verse 12 they were strangers to the commonwealth of Israel. *Strangers* means foreigners, meaning alien, and foreigners are people without the right of citizenship, which means they live in a place temporarily. Through Christ, they are no longer such but instead are fellow citizens, meaning native or possessing the same citizenship as the Jews. When people visit the U.S. from another country, they are temporarily living here. They have no rights of citizenship. Once they become citizens, they receive the same rights as the natives have.

So in Christ the Gentiles are no longer strangers and foreigners. They are no longer alienated and without rights. Paul says we are fellow citizens with the saints and we belong to the house or family of God. In other words, we belong to the same family as other believers. We are no longer on the outside looking in. We are no longer left out. Everybody who believes in Christ becomes fellow citizens and part of the family of God. So the Jews cannot force the Gentiles to go through certain rituals in order to be citizens and family members. When Christ died on the cross, what the Jews did became useless and has no effect for believers. Anybody who believes in Christ as Lord and Savior is part of the family of God, no matter who they are.

"And are built upon the foundation of the apostles and prophets, Jesus Christ Himself being the chief corner stone" (Eph. 2:20). The

Gentiles are built upon the foundation of the apostles and prophets. The foundation is the solid groundwork for the building. Since the Gentile believers are citizens and part of the family of God, they are built on the same foundation as the Jewish believers. The solid groundwork of the apostles and prophets is Jesus Christ. First Corinthians 3:11 says, "for other foundation can no man lay than that is laid, which is Jesus Christ." There is no other foundation that can be laid other than Jesus Christ. The apostles are the twelve disciples of Jesus Christ, excluding Judas Iscariot. The prophets are the New Testament prophets. These men helped build the church.

In Ephesians 4:11 Paul writes, "and he gave some, apostles; and some, prophets; and some, evangelists; and some, pastors and teachers." The apostles were the first to establish the church. The prophets were not sent ones like the apostles, and they had to conform to the apostles' teaching. Evangelists and pastor teachers replaced them. These men built on the foundation of Jesus Christ.

With Jesus as the chief cornerstone, they lined everything up according to Him. In other words, every stone that is laid on the foundation has to line up with the cornerstone. If anything is out of line, the building will not be square, which will throw the entire building off. Jesus is the cornerstone that the builders rejected (Ps. 118:22; Matt. 21:42; Mark 12:10–11; Luke 20:17– 18; Acts 4:11). Jesus said He would build the church (Matt. 16:18). Believers are being built upon the foundation of the apostles, with Jesus being the cornerstone. Both Jewish believers and Gentile believers are being built into the same building. The Jewish believers were built upon the foundation first, and now the Gentile believers are being included.

"In whom all the building fitly framed together groweth unto an holy temple in the Lord" (Eph. 2:21). "In whom" is referring to Jesus Christ. In Christ, the structure is organized compactly. This refers to the Jewish believers being framed together into a temple in the Lord.

The analogy continues into the next verse: "In whom ye also are builded together for an habitation of God through the Spirit" (Eph. 2:22). The Jewish believers are being organized compactly into a temple in the Lord, and so Paul adds that the Gentile believers are also being built into the same temple. The temple has several buildings, but it is joined together, and so is the church that is being built by Christ. Just as a company has different departments that are joined together under one roof, so is the church, with different buildings joined together by Jesus Christ, all working toward the same end. The temple has been built from different materials, but it constitutes one building. So is the church being built from different races, different backgrounds, and different parts of the world, but all are believers in Jesus Christ, and therefore they are all one building. All believers are stones being stacked upon the same foundation and fitted to the same cornerstone. We are all growing together for God's Spirit to dwell within. His dwelling is not in the building but in the believers. We are the body of Christ and are the true believers in Christ. "What? Know ye not that your body is the temple of the Holy Ghost which is in you, which ye have of God, and ye are not your own?"(1 Cor. 6:19) The church should not be built upon traditions and man's ideas. It should not be run like a business. The church is built upon the solid teaching of the foundation of the apostles and prophets, handed down from generation to generation.

Ephesians Chapter 3

Chapter 3 of Ephesians discusses Paul's stewardship. The secret of God's plan is hidden and revealed in verses 1–13; Paul's second prayer: to be strengthened, to be rooted and grounded in love, to comprehend, and to know the love of Christ appear in verses 14–21.

Ephesians 3:1 begins: "For this cause I Paul, the prisoner of Jesus Christ for you Gentiles." On this account, or for this reason, Paul is the prisoner of Jesus Christ for the Ephesians, who are Gentiles. Paul is the prisoner of Jesus Christ even though the Romans are the ones who hold him in chains. A prisoner is a captive, and Paul is captive because of the gospel he preached. It wasn't preaching in general that put him in bonds; it was about whom and to whom he was preaching. If he had preached to the Jews only, it would not have been a problem. If he had only preached the law, it wouldn't have been a problem. But when he said he was going to the Gentiles, the Jews wanted to kill him (Acts 22:21–22). When he preached Christ, the Jews opposed and reviled him (Acts 18:6). And the Jews contradicted Paul and his message (Acts 13:45) and even caused an uproar (Acts 17:5). Because of the jealousy of the Jews, Paul is a prisoner.

Paul is not complaining about his circumstances. What he has done for the Gentiles has caused him to be arrested and put in prison. He's not blaming the Gentiles; neither is he blaming God, as some would. God sent Paul to the Gentiles (Acts 9:15), and God was also going to show him how much he must suffer (Acts 9:16). Paul looked at these chains as a good thing if it meant people were being saved, and they were. Paul wrote to Timothy, "Therefore I endure all things for the elect's sake, that they may also obtain the salvation which is in Christ Jesus with eternal glory" (2 Tim. 2:10).

Paul doesn't finish the first verse of this chapter. He starts to say something but jumps on to something else. It is possible that he is picking up where he left off in verses 8, 13, or 14 in chapter 3. He needed to let the Gentiles know that he was imprisoned for their sakes. Paul didn't look at being in bonds as a devastating thing. He knew he was innocent of wrong. If Paul were devastated at this, he wouldn't have been able to pray and sing praises while in prison (Acts 16:25). Or, in the words of James, to count it all joy (James 1:2). Peter said, "If ye suffer for righteousness' sake, happy are ye: and be not afraid of their terror, neither be troubled; for it is better, if the will of God be so, that ye suffer for well doing, than for evil doing" (1 Pet. 3:14,17).

Paul continues: "If ye have heard of the dispensation of the grace of God which is given me to you-ward" (Eph. 3:2). "If you have heard" is saying if indeed or that he assumes they have heard of the dispensation of the grace of God given to him for them. *Dispensation* means the administration of a household or estate, management, or stewardship. In other words, Paul is handling the administration of God's grace, or favor.

Paul did not choose this for himself. Neither did he decide one day that he would like to be an apostle because it seemed like an easy way to make a living. God chose him for this ministry. Paul is a chosen vessel (Acts 9:15); he said a dispensation of the gospel was committed to him (1 Cor. 9:17), meaning God has entrusted him with His Word to handle it correctly. He was separated and called (Gal. 1:15); God separated him for this ministry and called him to it. He was made a minister according to the dispensation of God (Col. 1:25). God is the administrator, or manager, in calling Paul. Paul told Timothy that he was appointed a preacher, apostle, and a teacher to the Gentiles (2 Tim. 1:11). By the time, he wrote to the Ephesians, surely they had heard of the dispensation that God had given to him for them.

"How that by revelation He made known unto me the mystery; (as I wrote afore in few words, whereby, when ye read, ye may understand my knowledge in the mystery of Christ)" (Eph. 3:3–4). *Revelation* means uncovering or disclosure. It is uncovering the mystery, the purpose of God in this age. By revelation God is communicating things unknown. The book of Revelation is God's uncovering of future things, things previously unknown and revealed by God to the apostle John. Others have not known God's plans; God kept them secret until He decided to reveal them. Here Paul is referring to the salvation of the Gentiles and says God revealed His plan to Paul. It is Paul's purpose, as the administrator, to share this revelation with others. What is this secret? It is written in verse 6 of this chapter: the grace of God on the Gentiles that they would be one in Christ with the Jews. Paul says, "as I wrote afore in few words," meaning that he briefly wrote about God's mystery, which is referring to Ephesians 1:9–11 and 2:11–22.

When the Ephesian believers read this letter, they will be able to perceive the insight that Paul has into the mystery, or secret. Even now we can read Paul's insight into the mystery of Christ. So, Paul was the entrusted administrator to reveal to others what God had revealed to him. Paul could not keep this to himself. God entrusted Paul with His secrets, things that were unknown until God revealed them to Paul.

"Which in other ages was not made known unto the sons of men, as it is now revealed unto His holy apostles and prophets by the Spirit" (Eph. 3:5). "Which in other ages" refers to past generations. Paul does not mean that no one knew of the calling of the Gentiles to salvation; very few knew of it. The prophets knew it, but it was obscure and revealed by symbols. In past generations, men in general were not told of salvation of the Gentiles. Abraham was told that many would be blessed through him (Gen. 12:3). This means that men and women who believe in Christ are blessed through Abraham. It was through his seed that the Messiah came.

Paul said in Galatians 3:8, "And the scripture, foreseeing that God would justify the heathen through faith, preached before the gospel unto Abraham, saying, in thee shall all nations be blessed." This does not mean that we are blessed materially but rather that we are blessed spiritually, in that we have salvation through faith in Christ. The gospel was preached to Abraham long before the gospel was preached to others. Isaiah prophesied that He, Jesus, would be the light to the Gentiles (Isa. 49:6). What Paul is sharing with the Gentiles, people in past generations did not know; only the Old Testament prophets knew it.

Paul says the Spirit has now revealed it to His holy apostles and prophets. The mystery of the salvation of the Gentiles is now, during

Paul's time, being revealed. They are just now becoming aware of God's plans concerning the Gentiles. What the Old Testament prophets knew in part, vaguely, is now being revealed to the New Testament apostles. The apostles are now seeing God's plan unfolding, and they are seeing their part in His plan.

The apostles are the twelve, excluding Judas Iscariot; the prophets are the ones proclaiming God's Word with authority. The prophets' preaching had to conform to the apostles' teaching. They are the founders of the church (Eph. 4:11). God's plan for saving the Gentiles is being revealed to them by His Holy Spirit. In other words, what they know has come from the Lord through His Spirit.

"That the Gentiles should be fellow heirs, and of the same body, and partakers of His promise in Christ by the gospel" (Eph. 3:6). Here is the mystery made known. This is what was known in part in past generations, but it is now being revealed to the apostles and the prophets. The Gentiles should be joint heirs, or fellow participants; they should be part of the same body and be joint partakers, or coparticipants, of the promise of Christ through the gospel with the Jews. The Gentiles are now joint heirs. What was promised to Jewish believers is now promised to Gentile believers. They are to be part of the same body as the Jews, which is the body of Christ. The gospel is the good news, or the good message, and it is the good message of salvation in Christ. The gospel was preached to the Jews, and when they believed, they received salvation. The same goes for the Gentiles. There is one gospel, and it is the gospel of Jesus Christ.

"Whereof I was made a minister, according to the gift of the grace of God given unto me by the effectual working of His power" (Eph. 3:7). This verse is saying, of which, referring to the gospel, Paul became a servant according to the gift of the grace of God by God's active energy of His power. This leads us back to Eph. 3:2. It was for the gospel that he became a servant. It is to share the Word of God. Again, God called Paul to the ministry, and being entrusted with the revelation of God, Paul had to share it with others. If he did not share this mystery with others, he would not be a faithful servant. There is no greater honor than to be used by God to bring the gospel to the Gentiles. The same goes for men and women in the ministry who are called by God. If Paul would have known beforehand everything that would happen to him, he would not have changed a thing.

Paul says he was made a minister according to the gift of the grace of God. It was God's favor on Paul to call him into the ministry, to make him a servant. And it was the active energy of God's power that made him a servant. God worked in Paul's life to make him into who he was. It was God's active, productive energy that made Paul a servant. He is a servant of God and not of man. In Romans 15:15–16, he wrote: "Nevertheless, brethren, I have written the more boldly unto you in some sort, as putting you in mind, because of the grace that is given to me of God, that I should be the minister of Jesus Christ, ministering the gospel of God, that the offering up of the Gentiles might be acceptable, being sanctified by the Holy Ghost."

John Gill wrote he is a true minister of the gospel who is called of God to the work of the ministry, who is qualified by Him with grace and gifts for it, and who faithfully discharges it according to the ability God has given[1]. Matthew Henry wrote that what God calls men to He fits them for and does it with an almighty power[2]. It was God's grace or favor by His active, productive power that made Paul a servant of the gospel.

"Unto me, who am less than the least of all saints, is this grace given, that I should preach among the Gentiles the unsearchable riches of Christ" (Eph. 3:8). In this verse, Paul acknowledges God's grace in his life. He said in verse 2 that the dispensation is given to him by God's grace, meaning he is the steward of God by God's grace. In verse 7, he said he was made a servant by God's grace. Remember, grace is undeserved favor. It is by God's grace that he got to do what he did. So favor is given to him not based on what he has done and not because of who he is but because it is God's favor. It is God who allowed him to do what he did.

Paul said in 1 Corinthians, "For I am least of the apostles, that am not meet to be called an apostle, because I persecuted the church of God (15:9). Basically, Paul is saying that he is not even fit to be called

[1] John Gill, D.D., 1697-1771, John Gill's Exposition of the Entire Bible (Published in 1746-1766, 1816; public domain)
[2] Matthew Henry 1662-1712, Matthew Henry's Commentary volume 3 (London, 1845; public domain)

an apostle because he persecuted the church. He said to Timothy that he was "before a blasphemer, and a persecutor, and injurious" (1 Tim. 1:13). Paul was someone who spoke evil, using abusive language, like a persecutor, which can be read in Acts chapter 9. Paul was a violent, spiteful man.

The name Paul means little or small. To some, it would seem foolish for a man to think of himself as such when he is such a spiritual giant. Paul wrote over half of the New Testament. Why would he think of himself as the least of the apostles? He was lowering himself in order to lift other saints. Basically, he is saying there were other saints who deserved this grace to preach to the Gentiles. God did use other saints but in different ministries. But God gave the grace of preaching to the Gentiles to Paul. Paul thought of Peter, James, and John as pillars of the faith (Gal. 2:9), so wouldn't God use them instead? But Paul was the chosen vessel to the Gentiles.

Paul got to preach the unsearchable riches of Christ. That means the riches of Christ are beyond comprehension and untraceable. The riches of Christ are like outer space. Astronomers are constantly discovering new things in the galaxies or the Milky Way. They cannot explore everything out there; it is too vast. So it is with the riches of Christ. There is so much to know about Christ that Paul can only scratch the surface. And what he did know, he revealed to us. He wrote to the Romans, "O the depth of the riches both of the wisdom and knowledge of God! How unsearchable are his judgments, and his ways past finding out" (Rom.11:33)!

The book of Ephesians continues: "And to make all men see what is the fellowship of the mystery, which from the beginning of the world hath been hid in God, who created all things by Jesus Christ" (3:9). Not only is grace given to Paul to preach the unsearchable riches of Christ, but grace is also given to him to illuminate all men of the fellowship of the mystery. This is part of the dispensation given to Paul. He is to illuminate all of what is the partnership, or participation, of the mystery. This is what he has been doing in the last several verses: revealing all that God has revealed to him. He did that in Ephesians 1:9–10, too. Paul is to illuminate all men of God's plan, of the partnership of the Gentiles and the Jews.

To illuminate or enlighten is to explain, and explaining is what Paul has been doing. The mystery of God's plan for the Gentiles has been kept secret in God since the beginning of time. When all things were created through Jesus Christ, God decided to keep His plan of salvation of the Gentiles a secret until now, when He revealed it to Paul. All men, Jew and Gentile, are to know God's plan, and He used Paul to do it. Not even Peter, James, or John—Jesus's inner three—knew of God's plan for the Gentiles. God eventually revealed it to Peter in Acts 10. Not even the greatest of prophets knew of God's plan.

"To the intent that now unto the principalities and powers in heavenly places might be known by the church the manifold wisdom of God" (Eph. 3:10). God is revealing His plan for the Gentiles so that even the principalities and powers will know about it. Principalities are rulers, and powers are authorities. These are the angels in the heavenly places, or heaven. The angels did not know God's plan for the Gentiles. They did not know that God would eventually save the Gentiles.

God's wisdom is called manifold, meaning diverse or variety. Paul is saying that the purpose of this revelation is so the heavenly angels will know through the church God's wisdom. The church is the believing Jews and Gentiles, and the mystery is that both are one in Christ. God's wisdom is how He brought both together, which is through the cross. What was kept a secret from the beginning of time—the angels did not know, the prophets of old did not know, and the apostles didn't understand at first—is now revealed so that the angels will know. The angels will know through the Jews and Gentiles being one in Christ the wisdom of God. They will know God's plan, which He kept secret from the beginning of time. The prophets of old knew vaguely. Jesus had hinted at it to the disciples. But God revealed it to Paul. As a result, we have God's wisdom and secret written down so that we would know.

Paul wrote, "but unto them which are called, both Jews and Greeks, Christ the power of God, and the wisdom of God" (1 Cor. 1:24). Christ is the power of God, which brought both groups together. Christ is the wisdom of God; that is, Christ is how God brought them both together. The manifold wisdom of God is diverse, and it's like the riches of Christ: we cannot comprehend it. But through the church the angels will see what they didn't see at the beginning.

"According to the eternal purpose which He purposed in Christ Jesus our Lord" (Eph. 3:11). The plan was kept a secret from the beginning and was revealed in line with God's plan of the ages, which He accomplished through Jesus Christ. To make the Jews and Gentiles one through Christ was God's purpose from the beginning. He accomplished it through the cross. *Christ* means Anointed or Messiah, and *Jesus* means "Jehovah is salvation" or "Jehovah saved." *Lord* is supreme in authority. The only way to be saved is through Jesus Christ. Jesus is the Anointed One for men to be saved by God. God's eternal intention was for both Jews and Gentiles to be saved through Jesus Christ.

"In whom we have boldness and access with confidence by the faith of Him" (Eph. 3:12). *In whom*, meaning Jesus, we have both confidence and admission with trust through faith in Him. Only believers have confidence and admission with trust in Christ. Paul says, "wherefore I desire that ye faint not at my tribulations for you, which is your glory" (Eph. 3:13). This leads us back to verse 1, where Paul says he is the prisoner of Jesus Christ. He is asking that the Ephesians do not lose heart because of his afflictions for them. God used this to reveal to him His plans for the Gentiles. Things unknown from the beginning are now being revealed so that the Gentiles will know their place in God's plan.

Paul said to the Corinthians, "And whether we be afflicted, it is for your consolation and salvation, which is effectual in the enduring of the same sufferings which we also suffer: or whether we be comforted, it is for your consolation and salvation" (2 Cor. 1:6). No matter what happens to Paul, it is for their consolation and salvation. The same goes for the Ephesians. This is for their glory, which begins with salvation. The thousands and millions of men and women who risked their lives for the salvation of others, it is for the glory of the ones being saved. Paul is asking that they do not give up because of his afflictions. If he didn't preach the gospel, he wouldn't be in prison, and if he were not in prison, he wouldn't have received this revelation.

"For this cause I bow my knees unto the Father or our Lord Jesus Christ" (Eph. 3:14). After spending some time writing about his calling and ministry, Paul now goes back to his original thought from verse 1. When he says he bends his knees, it means he is praying for them. This is the second time he prays for them; the first is in Ephesians 1:16–19.

Paul bends his knees in submission and reverence, which was a common practice for people in those days. In the Old Testament, we can find examples of men who kneeled to pray and sometimes even raised their hands toward heaven. Solomon (1 Kings 8:54) and Ezra (9:5) are just two examples. A psalmist wrote, "O come, let us worship and bow down: let us kneel before the LORD our Maker" (Ps. 95:6). Daniel would kneel and pray three times a day (Dan. 6:10). Jesus prayed on His knees in the Garden of Gethsemane (Luke 22:41). Stephen prayed on his knees while being stoned (Acts 7:60). There are several other examples of kneeling and praying in Acts 20:36 and 21:5.

Paul says he bows his knees to the Father of our Lord Jesus Christ, showing the oneness of the Father and Son. God is the Father of our Lord Jesus Christ. Jesus is our Lord, meaning He is supreme in authority, and God is His Father. Since He is Jesus's Father, He is ours also. Paul's prayer is addressed to the Father, and when we pray, our prayers should be addressed to the Father, too. Jesus gave us a model to follow when we pray in Matthew 6:5–13. Jesus acknowledges God as His Father in this model prayer and in John 10:29–30 and 20:17. In John 3:16, Jesus told Nicodemus that God so loved the world that He gave His only begotten Son, which is Jesus Christ.

"Of whom the whole family in heaven and earth is named" (Eph. 3:15). "Of whom" is referring to God the Father. Every family is every class of men, no matter their race, gender, or age. This means that everyone who believes in Christ is in God's family. In Jesus Christ, we are all united, and He is above everything (Eph. 1:10, 21). In Galatians 3:26, Paul said, "for ye are all the children of God by faith in Christ Jesus." By believing in Jesus Christ, we are children of God.

"That He would grant you, according to the riches of His glory, to be strengthened with might by His Spirit in the inner man" (Eph. 3:16). Paul is praying for God to give them growth in strength with power through His Spirit. This is an example of intercessory prayer. Paul is praying on their behalf that they would grow in strength. Here is a man who is in prison for preaching the gospel interceding for others. The only thing he asks for them to pray for is for him to be bold in witnessing to others.

Paul is praying that God will give to them according to the riches, or wealth, of His glory, which is according to who God is. Paul's prayer is that God will give to them according to His wealth so that their inner man, or souls, may grow strong with power through His Spirit. Growing strong with power comes from the Holy Spirit working in the souls of the believers. He strengthens the inner man, and He is the power of God in the lives of believers. Certain foods give a person physical strength, and we all need those nutrients to make us strong. But here the believer needs the Holy Spirit to grow strong. Paul wrote to the Corinthians, "but though our outward man perish, yet the inward man is renewed day by day" (2 Cor. 4:16). The outward man is the physical body, and it decays as we age. The inward man is the soul, which is renewed day by day through the Holy Spirit. The body is temporal; the soul is eternal.

"That Christ may dwell in your hearts by faith; that ye, being rooted and grounded in love" (Eph. 3:17). The soul grows strong with might through the Holy Spirit so that Christ has a permanent place to call home. He is at home in the heart through belief. In this passage, "the heart" refers to the thoughts, passions, and desires of man, just to name a few. When Christ has a permanent home in the heart, nothing else resides there. When there is more than one person living in a home, they each have their stuff in their own rooms. Everything is separated as yours and mine. When more than one person lives in a house, they cannot really call it home; in other words, they cannot really get comfortable. They must share many things, and when one person moves out, that person takes his or her stuff and the other person is left with what he or she brought into the house. This analogy applies to people who share a house as roommates, not as a married couple or family.

Jesus Christ does not occupy one room in the heart; He is at home in the whole heart. So, when the Spirit strengthens the soul, He prepares the heart for Jesus to live there permanently. Even though the new believer has Christ living in the heart from the time he or she believes, he or she has many things that still occupy space there, so the Spirit must work to clean it out. When the soul is strengthened, Christ starts to have a permanent place to call home.

The strengthened soul is being rooted and grounded in love, meaning the believer is firmly fixed and established. Being rooted is like a tree: the deeper the roots, the stronger the tree. In Psalms 92:12–15, there is a poem that talks about how the Christian should be like a palm tree. The palm will not break under pressure, and the bark is resistant to damage. It will not burn, just like the Christian will not burn in hell. Long taproots like Christians should be rooted deep in God's Word. The older the palm, the sweeter its fruits. The palm has more than eight hundred uses, and it grows from the inside, out as Christians should grow from the heart. The righteous shall flourish as the palm.

Being grounded means having a foundation. Just as a building needs a foundation to be established, so does the Christian. Sometimes a building with a solid foundation is dug into the ground and built upon a rock (Luke 6:48). Paul says they are rooted and grounded in love, referring to their love for Jesus Christ. If the Spirit is strengthening the inner man so that Christ may have a place to call home in the heart, then they are rooted deep and built upon the solid foundation of Christ and have a love for Him. This love is demonstrated by action. We love Christ by obeying His Words. That is illustrated by the parable of the builder. We love Jesus Christ by obeying His commands (John 14:15, 21, 23; 2 John 6).

"May be able to comprehend with all saints what is the breadth, and length, and depth, and height; and to know the love of Christ, which passeth knowledge, that ye might be filled with all the fulness of God" (Eph. 3:18–19). Paul not only prays that God will strengthen the soul so that Christ may have a place to call home and that they would be rooted and grounded, but he also he prays that they will have enough strength to grasp the width, length, depth, and height and to know the love of Christ. This comes in stages. First is the strengthening of the inner man. Second, Christ has a permanent place to call home. Third, being rooted and grounded in love for the Lord. And fourth, that they are able to fully take hold and understand the love of God.

Paul says so they would comprehend with all saints; that means other believers. Believers should know how wide, long, deep, and high the love of God is. Paul describes the love of God in dimensions to give them a mental picture of how big His love is. He prays that they may fully understand the love of God and His love toward them. Paul says they should know this love, which exceeds knowledge. This kind of knowledge is experiential knowledge. When we experience this kind of love, it excels just knowledge of it. People can describe what love is when someone asks, but that is just knowledge, meaning that is just to know mentally of it. But when they experience the love that has been explained, then it surpasses just knowing about it to experiencing it themselves. We can know the love of Christ by reading about it in Scripture or hearing testimonies from others. But to know the love of Christ is to experience it yourself because God has called us from a life of sin. This is not a sentimental, warm, fuzzy, puppy love kind of love; it is love demonstrated on the cross and God calling us through His Spirit unto salvation.

Action demonstrates this kind of love. "God commendeth His love toward us, in that, while we were yet sinners, Christ died for us." (Rom. 5:8). "In this was manifested the love of God toward us, because God sent His only begotten Son into the world that we might live through Him. Herein is love, not that we loved God, but that He loved us, and sent His Son to be the propitiation for our sins" (1 John 4:9–10). It was the love of God that moved Frederick Lehman to write the hymn "The Love of God." The result is to be filled with the fullness of God. It is to be filled to the top, to be stuffed, yet desiring to take in more.

"Now unto Him that is able to do exceeding abundantly above all that we ask or think, according to the power that worketh in us" (Eph. 3:20). Here Paul means now unto God who is able to do exceedingly over and above all that we ask or comprehend. Whatever we ask God to do, He is able to do exceedingly over and above that. Whatever we comprehend God can do, He is able to do exceedingly over and above that. This is according to the power that is the Holy Spirit working in us. With the Holy Spirit active and operative in us, God can do exceedingly over and above all that we ask or think.

"Unto Him be glory in the church by Christ Jesus throughout all ages, world without end. Amen" (Eph. 3:21). To God be the honor and praise for His ability to do exceedingly over and above all that we ask or comprehend, according to the power that is active in us. In other words, glory to God in the church within Jesus unto all generations of the age of the ages. Amen, or so be it or let it be fulfilled. May God answer Paul's prayers concerning the Ephesian believers, He who is able to do exceedingly over and above what Paul thinks or asks.

Ephesians Chapter 4

Ephesians chapters 4–6 cover the duties of the believers, meaning the life application of what has been taught in chapters 1–3, including their walk toward one another (the unity and gifts in the church) in verses 1–16 and their walk toward unbelievers (old man and new man and commandments) in verses 17–32.

"I therefore, the prisoner of the Lord, beseech you that ye walk worthy of the vocation wherewith ye are called" (Eph. 4:1). Paul again is saying that he is the prisoner of the Lord. In Ephesians chapter 3, he says he is the prisoner of Jesus Christ. Paul is the prisoner of Jesus Christ our Lord. Paul is not a prisoner by accident, and as we saw in the previous chapter, God was able to use this imprisonment to reveal to Paul His plans concerning the Gentiles. If Paul looked at this as a prisoner of the Romans, he would probably be moaning and complaining. But since he is a captive of the Lord, he can make the most of the situation by encouraging believers through letters. He also used this opportunity to witness to the Roman soldiers and other nonbelievers. All the people who were held captives for preaching the gospel looked at their imprisonment as an opportunity, not as victims of circumstance. With Jesus having supreme authority in Paul's life, what does he have to complain about? He is doing the work of the Lord, not his own.

Paul starts this chapter by urging the believers to live suitably to their calling. The word *vocation* is not vocation as we think of it; this is not a job or a career. The word *vocation* here is the calling to salvation. In the introduction, we read that the first three chapters of the book of Ephesians address doctrine; doctrine is instruction. So now the next three chapters cover life application. Our salvation is a holy calling, as Paul told Timothy in 2 Timothy 1:9. In other words, our calling to salvation is not of us. We are called with a holy calling, and we are to be different. Peter said, "But as He which hath called you is holy, so be ye holy in all manner of conversation; because it is written, be ye holy; for I am holy" (1 Pet. 1:15–16). As we are called with a holy calling, we are to live, or behave, accordingly. No matter where we are in our lives, no matter the circumstances in which we find ourselves, we are to live suitably to our calling. In the next few verses, Paul addresses how the Ephesians are to live suitably according to that calling.

"With all lowliness and meekness, with longsuffering, forbearing one another in love; endeavoring to keep the unity of the Spirit in the bond of peace" (Eph. 4:2–3). Paul is telling them what is involved in this calling. Since the calling is a holy calling, there are some guidelines that need to be followed. The believer is not left in this world without any knowledge of how to live as Christ. When God called the Israelites from Egypt, He gave them rules and regulations that set them apart from other nations. It is the law, which included the Ten Commandments.

To begin this, Paul mentions lowliness and meekness. Lowliness is humility, a thinking low of oneself. Not low as in "I'm a worm" type of thinking, but thinking low to lower oneself in order to lift others. The Scripture talks about being humble. Moses was humbler than any man on the earth (Num. 12:3). In Psalms, it reads, "though the LORD be high, yet hath He respect unto the lowly: but the proud He knoweth afar off" (Ps. 138:6). God sees the humble, but the proud He knows from a distance. He is nowhere near the proud. In Proverbs, it is written, "Better it is to be of an humble spirit with the lowly, than to divide the spoil with the proud" (Prov. 16:19). In Philippians 2:3, Paul said in lowliness of mind let each other esteem the other better than themselves. Meekness is to be gentle with others, and it also involves humility. If believers are to live suitably to their calling, this is how we need to live. When we are humble in mind and gentle, that's when we have patience.

Longsuffering means to be patient with people. We are not all the same, and if we were, this would be a boring place to live because everybody would have the same temperament. Along with patience comes putting up with others in love. This means to tolerate other people. By that I don't mean tolerate people who are sinful or living in sin, but rather tolerate people because everybody is different. If we are to be patient with people, we must tolerate them also.

Paul says that they must try to maintain, or guard, the unity of the Spirit. The Spirit of God united us, and we are to maintain that unity, or oneness. If we are to live suitably to our calling as believers, we must maintain that unity. Humility, preferring another over oneself, being gentle, being patient, and putting up with one another in love, is what that maintains the unity in the bond of peace.

The bond is what binds together. To be in peace here is to be in harmony. To be in harmony is what binds us together. Jesus prayed that all believers would be one (John 17:21–23). Paul said to the Corinthians, "Now I beseech you, brethren, by the name of our Lord Jesus Christ, that ye all speak the same thing, and that there be no divisions among you; but that ye be perfectly joined together in the same mind and in the same judgment" (1 Cor. 1:10). He is urging the believers in Corinth to be united and to be complete in the same mind and of same opinion, or resolve.

"There is one body, and one Spirit, even as ye are called in one hope of your calling; one Lord, one faith, one baptism, one God and Father of all, who is above all, and through all, and in you all" (Eph. 4:4–6). Here is the life application for Ephesians 2:16 and 3:6. In those verses, Paul was talking about Jews and Gentiles being one, or united in Christ. This goes for all believers in Jesus Christ. There is one body, which is the body of Christ, the church; there is one Spirit, which is the Holy Spirit; and there is one hope, which is the confident expectation of our calling to salvation. One hope of salvation is in Christ. One Lord, that is Jesus Christ, who is supreme in authority. One faith, which is the belief in Christ, that is the Christian faith, only one faith in Jesus Christ. One baptism, which is immersion, just as Jesus did at His baptism and so we follow. Baptism signifies that the person has believed Christ as his Lord and Savior and so follows Him in believers' baptism.

One God and Father of all does not mean that God is the Father of all people; instead it means one God and Father of all believers in Christ (Gal. 3:26). There is only one God and Father of all. He is over all and through all and in all, meaning He is in believers through the Holy Spirit. Just as these are all one, so are the believers in Jesus Christ. That means no matter their race, gender, age, or nationality, when people believe in Jesus Christ as Lord and Savior, they become one with other believers in Christ.

"But to each one of us is given grace according to the measure of the gift of Christ" (Eph. 4:7). Even though all believers are one, each believer has grace given to him or her. What does Paul mean by grace given? He means that each believer is given favor to work in some ministry. All believers are one, but to each of them is given a different grace. Paul mentioned what his grace was in Ephesians 3:2, 8. Each believer has something given to him or her according to the portion of the gift of Christ, and each portion is different. There can be more than one person in the church with the same grace, but they use it in different ways. It is the gift of Christ, meaning it is given freely to believers.

"Wherefore He saith, when He ascended up on high, He led captivity captive, and gave gifts unto men. (Now that He ascended, what is it but that He also descended first into the lower parts of the earth? He that descended is the same also that ascended up far above all heavens, that He might fill all things)" (Eph. 4:8–10). In these verses, Paul quotes from Psalms 68:18: "Thou hast ascended on high, Thou hast led captivity captive: Thou hast received gifts for men; yea, for the rebellious also, that the LORD God might dwell among them." This is what military leaders would do over their enemies. They would take their spoils and give them out as gifts among themselves. David did this, as recorded in 1 Samuel 30:26, and the king in Esther 2:18 did as well. Paul is saying that when Christ ascended up to the heights, He led a multitude of captives; that is, He made prisoners of war out of the captives.

When Christ returned in victory over death, He gave gifts unto men. In Psalms, it is written that He received gifts for men. This shows that Jesus had the right to share these gifts as He pleased, just as a conqueror had the right to share the spoils with others as he pleased. In the parenthesis, Paul adds now that He ascended, referring to Jesus ascending to Heaven, what is it except He descended to the grave, referring to Jesus's death and burial. This portion could be expounding on Jesus's ascension and leading captives' captive. Paul is saying that Jesus had to first suffer death before He could ascend to the heights. Before men could receive their gifts, Jesus had to first descend to the grave and then ascend to the heights. Paul is showing how Christ is victorious over death and the grave through His resurrection.

Him leading captivity captive could refer to the dead saints rising from the grave at the resurrection of Christ. They had been held captive by the grave for many years and had now been released. He led captivity captive by His defeat over death, the grave, and Satan by His power over them. Some say He led captivity captive, which is sin, death, and the curse of the law. No matter the interpretation, Paul is saying that Jesus first came down to earth, suffered, and died and that He is victorious over these things by His resurrection. Jesus told Nicodemus that no man had ascended to heaven but the one who came down from heaven (John 3:13). He who descended is the same as He who ascended greatly higher than the universe. Read Ephesians 1:20–23.

He did these things to completely fulfill all things. What things? All the prophecies concerning Jesus (Luke 24:44), including His death, resurrection, and His mercy to the Gentiles. The last things He added to fulfill are the gifted men mentioned in the next verse.

"And He gave some, apostles; and some, prophets; and some, evangelists; and some, pastors and teachers" (Eph. 4:11). Jesus gave the apostles, the prophets, the evangelists, and the pastor-teacher. Apostles established the church. They are sent by Jesus Christ. They received and proclaimed the Word of God. Their qualifications include seeing the resurrected Christ and performing miracles, just to name a few. Prophets also established the church and preached the Word of God. They worked in the local congregations, and their message had to conform to the apostles' teaching. The offices of apostle and prophet do not exist today. Evangelists preach the good news. They travel and preach the gospel and are sometimes referred to as missionaries. Pastors feed the local flock. Teachers teach and pastor. Teaching means to feed and educate the local congregation. All these gifted men were given to the church, and they were to build the church not in their ability but in the power of Christ working through them.

"For the perfecting of the saints, for the work of the ministry, for the edifying of the body of Christ" (Eph. 4:12). Paul explains why the Lord gave the apostles, prophets, evangelists, pastor-teacher. It was to equip, fit, furnish, or prepare the saints, who are believers of performing service and building up the church. All believers should be serving the Lord, and these men equipped them to do it. When all believers are serving, then it will build up the church. The apostles, prophets, evangelists, pastor-teachers are to fit the believers for service. The apostles and prophets laid the foundation of the church, which is upon Jesus Christ. The evangelist preaches the gospel of Jesus Christ to lost people. The pastor-teacher feed and tend the flock, which is the local congregation. They all work together to equip the believers to the work of ministry, and the goal is to build up the church. Basically, all these men equipped believers. Peter's commission was to feed the Lord's sheep (John 21:15–17). In chapters 9, 11, and 14 of the book of Acts, the churches were edified, equipped with believers, and encouraged. They passed on to the next set of leaders what they had learned.

"Till we all come in the unity of the faith, and of the knowledge of the Son of God" (Eph. 4:13). Paul also tells the Ephesians that this is to continue until we all arrive into the unity of the faith. The apostles and prophets have done what they were called to do. Evangelists continue to preach the gospel to the lost. The pastor-teacher are to continue feeding and tending to the flock. They are to continue until we all arrive to the unity of the faith; that is, continue until all come to faith in Jesus Christ. There is no end to this work. Even though the apostles and prophets have finished, the evangelists, pastor-teachers still have work to do. They still have believers to equip to the work of the ministry and to the building up of the church.

The knowledge of the Son of God means to have true knowledge of Jesus Christ. This means having a full or precise knowledge of Christ. Evangelists preach the gospel, which is about Jesus Christ and His work. Pastor-teachers teach believers what is written in the Word of God, which leads people to a full knowledge of Christ. This began with salvation, and it should continue to the next generation and be passed on to other faithful men who will in turn pass it on to other faithful men.

The rest of the verse reads, "Unto a perfect man, unto the measure of the stature of the fulness of Christ" (Eph. 4:13). To have us all arrive into the unity of the faith, to have full knowledge of Jesus Christ, should make believers into complete, or spiritually mature, believers. The perfecting or equipping, of the saints is to make them full-grown, mature believers. The teaching of the apostles and prophets, the preaching of the evangelists, and the shepherding of the pastor-teachers are to make full-grown believers.

"Into the portion of the maturity of the fullness of Christ" means Jesus Christ is our standard for spiritual maturity. The fullness of Christ is to be like Christ. The full knowledge of Christ should lead the believer to be like Him. The purpose of the teachings from those gifted men is for believers to be united, to be mature, and to be like Jesus Christ. To be fully mature in Christ takes a lifetime, and it cannot be fully done while here on earth.

"That we henceforth be no more children, tossed to and fro, and carried about with every wind of doctrine" (Eph. 4:14). *Children* refers to those unable to speak. This does not mean they cannot speak but rather that they are not at the age of speaking. Paul is making reference to the reason believers need to be mature. With these gifted men doing what God had called them to do, till we all come to unity and full knowledge of Christ, mature believers will not be tossed to and fro and carried about with every wind of doctrine. This means that mature believers have that full knowledge of Christ which makes them grounded. Having a full knowledge of Christ means that mature believers will know the difference between true doctrine and false doctrine. Paul says "tossed to and fro," meaning that just as waves surge, so do immature believers. Just as waves are sometime high and other times low, so it is with immature believers, meaning they are unstable. Unstable believers bounce from one teaching to another. They go from one trend to another based on what these teachers teach, and they hang on every word. As a result, they do not grow to be mature believers.

They are carried around by false teaching and lack the conviction of truth. Doctrine is teaching, or instruction, and when false teachers come, they lead immature Christians astray through their false teachings. Being unstable in conviction of truth leads immature Christians to be carried around by false teachings. Paul warned against this in Acts 20:30–31. We can read Romans 16:17–18 to see what Paul said about false teachers. Paul warned the Corinthians (2 Cor. 11:3–4), the Galatians (Gal. 1:6–7; 3:1), and the Colossians (Col. 2:4–8), and the writer of

Hebrews warned his readers (Heb. 13:9) of false teachers. Peter did the same (2 Pet. 2:1–3), as did the apostle John (1 John 2:19, 26; 4:1).

"By the sleight of men, and cunning craftiness, whereby they lie in wait to deceive" (Eph. 4:14). These false teachers defraud and deceive others. They are compared to dice players and are sometimes accustomed to cheating. Cheating is what they do to immature believers who lack knowledge of Jesus Christ. They disguise themselves to mislead people. They tend to deceive others. Paul is saying that just as men wait to ambush people, so do false teachers; they look for people they can mislead. They have a method with which they mislead unstable believers.

"But speaking the truth in love, may grow up into Him in all things, which is the head even Christ" (Eph. 4:15). They are to deal truthfully, or to act true, meaning be sincere in love. They must be real and genuine. They must not be like the false teachers who cheat people out of spiritual maturity. The false teachers live a lie when they make the appearance of godliness but teach false doctrine. They don't deal in love; all they want is a following. To live sincerely is to live one way in public and the same way in private. We are to live by the truth, which is the Word of God, especially if we are to grow in Christ in every way. This means we are to know the truth and to live according to it in every area of our lives. This includes loving to live according to the truth.

That they may grow into Jesus Christ in all things. With these words, Paul is reminding them that Jesus is the head, which means Jesus is the leader in the church, not man. Signs of childishness include selfishness and pride, and it keeps believers from growing into full-grown believers.

"From whom the whole body fitly joined together and compacted by that which every joint supplieth, according to the effectual working in the measure of every part, maketh increase of the body unto the edifying of itself in love" (Eph. 4:16). From whom, referring to Jesus Christ, the head, the whole body is framed together and united through the supply of each ligament, according to the active energy in the portion of each part, makes increase of the body unto the building up of itself in love. What does this mean? The body is the church; believers are framed together and united, as Paul already stated in Ephesians 2:21, and every part of the body needs one another to function and grow. Read 1 Corinthians 12:12–28 and Colossians 2:19.

Every part of the physical body is framed together and united. Everything is attached somehow. And every part supplies the next part, and when everything is working together, it will grow. Paul is comparing the church to the physical body. It needs every member to work together for the church to grow. The church gets its life from the head, which is Jesus Christ, and He supplies the body with all it needs to survive. When believers actively work—that is, do their parts—the body will grow into the building up of itself in love. Their love for one another will grow, and their love for one another will build up each other.

"This I say therefore, and testify in the Lord, that ye henceforth walk not as other Gentiles walk, in the vanity of their mind" (Eph. 4:17). "This I say therefore" is Paul picking up where he left off in verses 1–3 of this chapter: this I say so you will know how to walk, or live. The Ephesians know now how they are supposed to live, and the Lord Jesus is his witness that he has told them. They are without excuse and cannot claim they didn't know.

Since they now know how to live, they are no longer to live as other Gentiles. Remember, Gentiles are non-Jews, but in this case Paul is referring to Gentiles as unbelievers. So, you have Gentiles as non-Jewish people and as unbelievers, meaning pagan. Since the Ephesian believers have a new life, they are to live differently. Paul says that the other Gentiles live in the vanity of their mind, meaning their minds are corrupt. It shows the emptiness of their minds. But we must remember also that we used to live in that same condition (Eph. 2:1–3). Paul is saying that other Gentiles—that is, unbelievers—are morally corrupt in their minds. Paul did not only tell the Ephesians these things; he also told the Romans (Rom. 1:23–32), the Corinthians (1 Cor. 6:9–11), the Galatians (5:19–21), and the Colossians (Col. 3:5–8). Peter also reminded believers how they used to live (1 Pet. 4:3–4).

Paul describes them as "having the understanding darkened" (Eph. 4:18), meaning the mental power of the mind is darkened; in other words, there is no light. Their intelligence is darkened, and they cannot understand spiritual things. Their minds cannot comprehend these things because it is darkened and they are in their sins.

Paul also says, "being alienated from the life of God through the ignorance that is in them" (Eph. 4:18). This means the other Gentiles are shut out, or foreigners, from the life of God because of their ignorance. Paul said that the Gentiles in general were once alienated from the commonwealth of Israel, but because of what Jesus Christ did for them, they are now part of the commonwealth of Israel (Eph. 2:12). But what makes the Ephesians part of the commonwealth of Israel is that they believed in Jesus Christ. Believing is what set them apart from the other Gentiles. Paul is saying that because of their (the unbelieving Gentile's) ignorance, they have no life from God. This ignorance does not mean they are stupid, it just means they do not know what condition they are in. They have no spiritual life in them, which comes from God.

"Because of the blindness of their heart" (Eph. 4:18), meaning through the hardness of their hearts, they cannot understand spiritual things. Their ignorance is keeping them from the life of God, and it is because of the hardness of their hearts. When skin is calloused, it has lost feeling, and so it is with the heart that is hard: it has no feeling. Basically, they are not convicted of sin, so they refuse to change. As a result, they remain as unbelievers.

"Who being past feeling have given themselves over to lasciviousness, to work all uncleanness with greediness" (Eph. 4:19). In other words, they have become void of feeling; they are insensible. They have given themselves up to unbridled lust. This unbridled lust usually means they have a hatred of morality. Not only was this behavior known back then but in many ways it seems more visible today. It is immoral, impure, and sinful, and constitutes improper behavior and living. This type of person is someone who refuses to acknowledge any moral restraints and who acts upon his or her immoral impulses.

Living this way is a habit for these people, and they do it wanting more. It's like a trade or job. It's like second nature to them, as the saying goes. Job says men drink iniquity like water (Job 15:16); Isaiah said they are like greedy dogs that can never have enough (Isa. 56:11); Peter said they are like natural brute beasts—instinctive, irrational animals (2 Pet. 2:12). Paul warns them, and us, not to live like this in Ephesians 4:17.

Paul says, "But ye have not so learned Christ" (Eph. 4:20). This means they were not taught to live in their sins. Basically, they are to live differently by living according to the truth of the Word of God. Read Titus 2:11–14 to get an idea of how believers should live. Paul said to the Romans, "What shall we say then? Shall we continue in sin, that grace may abound? God forbid. How shall we, that are dead to sin, live any longer therein" (Rom. 6:1–2). In the gospel of Luke it says repentance and remissions of sins should be preached in His name among all nations (24:47).

"If so be that ye have heard Him, and have been taught by Him, as the truth is in Jesus" (Eph. 4:21). "If so be that" does not mean doubting. It means no doubt that you have heard Him. Indeed, not only have you heard Him but also been taught and instructed in Him. How have we heard Him? Read John 1:1–3, 14. Paul is saying that you have heard the Word of God taught. We can go back to read Ephesians 1:13. "As the truth is in Jesus" means truth is Jesus (John 14:6). The Ephesians have heard the gospel and responded to it. They have changed their lives by believing in Christ, repenting of their sins, and living for Christ. And because they have new lives, they are not to live as other Gentiles. The gospel has been preached from generation to generation, so we have heard the same message as the Ephesians. Believers didn't just learn about Christ; we applied His teaching to our lives. We have heard Him through the preaching and teaching of His Word.

"That ye put off concerning the former conversation the old man, which is corrupt according to the deceitful lusts" (Eph. 4:22). Paul is making reference to changing clothes. They are to throw off the old, filthy clothes, which is the behavior of the former life. The former life is morally decaying because of seducing desires, and the Ephesians are to throw it off.

"And be renewed in the spirit of your mind" (Eph. 4:23). This means to have a new mind. So when we throw off the old, former, sinful life, we should have a new mind. The believer's mind is not like the other Gentiles' minds, as in verse 17. In the book of Romans, Paul said not to be conformed to this world but to be transformed by the renewing of your mind (12:2), which means our minds should be thinking of things of Christ and His Word.

So, if the believer throws off the old former self, then he or she must put on something new. Paul says, "that ye put on the new man, which after God is created in righteousness and true holiness" (Eph. 4:24). This new man is a new nature, one that is created by God in righteousness and holiness of truth. Remember, in Ephesians 2:10 Paul said we are His workmanship, created in Christ Jesus unto good works. This does not mean a remodeled or renovated nature. That's what you get in a twelve-step program for addiction. That just changes your attitude toward that addiction. This means a new nature, something that is different. It is something in which people can see a difference. This new nature is created to walk in righteousness and true holiness according to the Word of God. It is God's standard, not man's.

"Wherefore putting away lying, speak every man truth with his neighbor: for we are members one of another" (Eph. 4:25). This putting away is the same as in verse 22, and it means to throw off. Since they have put on the new man and thrown off the old, the lie, or falsehood, is thrown off also. Since they are to throw off the falsehood, the practice of lying, each man is to speak truth with his neighbor. Paul told the Colossians, "Lie not one to another, seeing that ye have put off the old man with his deeds" (Col. 3:9). This deed has been thrown off with the old man, and it should not be a habit of the new man. Paul gives us the reason we should speak truth to one another: we are members of one another. Believers are members of one another; that is, we are part of the body of Christ. The command here is to speak to one another in truth. And it is also one of the Ten Commandments (Exod. 20:16). This here in Ephesians is the first of things listed that the new man should be doing.

"Be ye angry, and sin not: let not the sun go down upon your wrath" (Eph. 4:26). This type of anger is not because you didn't get your way. This is a righteous anger when you are wronged. This is a permissive, or a positive, command to be angry. Then comes the negative command to sin not. We all get angry sometimes, and it is okay. Anger is to be a passing emotion, meaning it shouldn't continue. When we let that anger continue to dwell in us, we sin. This comes from Psalm 4:4: "Stand in awe, and sin not: commune with your own heart upon your bed, and be still. Selah." The psalmist says to quiver with anger but do not sin. Do not let that emotion get out of control. In Proverbs, the writer talked about anger several times (14:29; 19:11; 25:23). James encourages us to be slow to speak and slow to wrath (James 1:19).

But also do not let the sun go down on your wrath or rage, which is a settled state of mind. This, too, is another command. This leads to bitterness and hatred toward someone. Paul also says, "neither give place to the devil" (Eph. 4:27), which means do not give the devil an opportunity. If we remain in a state of wrath, then we have given an opportunity for the devil to operate. Paul tells us to put on the whole armor of God so we can stand against the wiles of the devil (Eph. 6:11). James tells us to resist the devil (James 4:7). And Peter tells us to be sober and vigilant because the devil is seeking whom he may devour (1 Pet. 5:8).

"Let him that stole steal no more: but rather let him labor, working with his hands the thing which is good, that he may have to give to him that needeth" (Eph. 4:28). Thou shalt not steal is another of the Ten Commandments (Exod. 20:15). Paul is saying to let him who stole labor, working hard, being engaged in work, which is good. As someone once said, hard work has never killed anyone. Solomon wrote in Proverbs that he who gathers by labor shall increase (13:11) and in all labor, there is profit (14:23). God has intended us to work, and work was enjoyable before sin entered. We can read in the book of Genesis of when God placed Adam in the garden to work it, but when he sinned, work became a curse (Gen. 2:15; 3:17–19). The purpose of working is so that we can give to someone in need.

"Let no corrupt communication proceed out of your mouth, but that which is good to the use of edifying, that it may minister grace unto the hearers" (Eph. 4:29). This is a reference to rotten fruit or a dead animal, which is ugly, bad, and disgusting. So this means we are not to let any rotten or defiling speech come out of our mouths. Paul will bring this up again in Ephesians chapter 5. Instead, what should come out of the new man's mouth is that which is good to the occasion of building up so that it may give grace to those who hear. This means to edify profitably. It is to edify others toward spiritual maturity.

There are times when people need to hear something edifying out of someone else's mouth. There is enough corrupt talk around without believers adding to it. Some believers will carry on with those who are not believers; that is, they will talk just as corruptly as unbelievers. We cannot expect to build somebody up when we are talking just like unbelievers. These people give Christ a bad name, it makes them look like hypocrites, and others criticize them. Not only that, but they also destroy other new believers. So, believers should talk in a way that causes other believers to grow in grace.

"And grieve not the Holy Spirit of God, whereby ye are sealed unto the day of redemption" (Eph. 4:30). The most known case of God being grieved is with the Israelites in the wilderness (Heb. 3:17). When believers sin, they grieve the Holy Spirit, meaning they cause Him pain. Paul told the Thessalonians, "quench not the Spirit" (1 Thess. 5:19), meaning do not extinguish the Spirit by sin. Paul reminded the Ephesians that the Holy Spirit seals them unto the day of redemption (Eph. 1:13–14). God's Spirit is the stamp on the believer, meaning that we are His, and His promise is through His Spirit that we will be ransomed from this age and into the presence of the Lord. We grieve His Spirit, who is our promise that we are His, when we willfully sin against God.

"Let all bitterness, and wrath, and anger, and clamour, and evil speaking, be put away from you, with all malice" (Eph. 4:31). It is typical for Paul to use the word *and* between words. He uses *and* as emphasis to make all the words important. One is not worse than the other, but all are as bad as the other. They all spring forth from one another. Bitterness is like poison. Doctors have shown that if a person harbors bitterness, their health goes downhill. Bitterness is bitter hatred, and it is bitterness in spirit and speech. Wrath is inward anger that displays itself. It is anger that explodes and then subsides. Anger is a settled state of mind with the possibility of taking revenge. We read earlier, be ye angry and sin not. Yes, it is natural to be angry, but we need to not dwell on it and should put it away from us before we settle on it. Clamor is uproar or an outcry. It is uproar of controversy. Evil speaking is the same as slander or to verbally injure another's name. This includes malice, which is the root of these sins. Malice is ill will or injurious. When there is malice, you'll have these other sins. All these sins grieve the Holy Spirit. Deeds of the old man should be thrown off when the believer puts on the new man.

And the opposite of these words comes next: "and be ye kind one to another, tenderhearted, forgiving one another, even as God for Christ's sake hath forgiven you" (Eph. 4:32). Being kind to someone is being good or useful to him or her. This is the opposite of bitterness.

Tenderheartedness is having sympathy toward another, which is the opposite of wrath. Forgiveness is the opposite of anger. To show forgiveness to someone is to show favor upon that person. Basically, it means not holding a grudge against someone because he or she has done you wrong.

God has forgiven us for Christ's sake. God has shown us favor in Christ. And because God has shown us favor, we should show others favor. Jesus told us that if we will not forgive others, God will not forgive us (Matt. 6:14–15). Before that Jesus said forgive our debts as we forgive our debtors (Matt. 6:12). Paul told the Romans, "Therefore if thine enemy hunger, feed him; if he thirst give him drink: for in so doing thou shalt heap coals of fire on his head. Be not overcome of evil, but overcome evil with good" (Rom. 12:20–21). The new man is tenderhearted, kind, and forgiving, just as God forgave us.

Ephesians Chapter 5

Chapter 5 of the book of Ephesians calls upon readers to be imitators of God. The call to walk in love, purity and prudence, light and dark, wise and unwise is covered in verses 1–21, and Spirit-filled believers conduct, specifically between husbands and wives is addressed in verses 22–33.

"Be ye therefore followers of God, as dear children" (Eph. 5:1). To follow God is to be an imitator, or to copy Him. Here, Paul is continuing from the last two verses in chapter 4. If we imitate or copy God, we will not live in those sins previously mentioned and instead will live out the command to be kind, tenderhearted, and forgiving. How do we know how to imitate God? By reading His Word. Leviticus 11:45 discusses His holiness; Matthew 5:44 talks of love and mercy; Luke 6:35-36 talks of love and mercy; 1 Peter 1:15-16 talks of holiness; 1 John 4:11 also talks of loving one another. Paul encouraged others to imitate him because he was imitating Jesus Christ. Paul tells the Ephesians to follow God as dear children. Believers are beloved children of God.

"And walk in love, as Christ also hath loved us, and hath given Himself for us an offering and a sacrifice to God for a sweetsmelling savour" (Eph. 5:2). Jesus commands us to love one another (John 13:34), and as God loves us, so should we love others. Paul told us to do all things in love (1 Cor. 16:14). So, this means it is not a feeling type of love; it is an act of love, a demonstration of love. If love were based on feelings, then it would be different things to different people. Love is a verb, as the old song goes. John said we should love one another not as Cain, who killed his brother (1 John 3:11–12). Also, John wrote that if we say we love God and hate our brother, we are liars (1 John 4:20).

We are to walk in love, as Christ loved us by giving Himself for us.

Jesus said He gave His life to ransom us (Matt. 20:28). He also said there is no greater love than for a man to lay down his life for his friends (John 15:13). Jesus was willing to give His life for us. That is love demonstrated by Him. Jesus did that to deliver us from our sin. If you love someone, wouldn't you be willing to keep him or her from disaster? We warn our children of dangers because we love them. So Jesus gave His life to deliver us from the wrath to come when God brings judgment on sinful men.

The apostle John wrote, "Hereby perceive we the love of God because He laid down His life for us: and we ought to lay down our lives for the brethren" (1 John 3:16). Herein we know the love of Christ by His death. And because of His life-giving love, we should be willing to lay down our lives for the brethren. We should be willing to give up ourselves for the brethren. This includes the giving of our time, care, labors, prayers, and substance. We cannot lay down our lives for the brethren as Christ did, meaning redeeming the brethren; only Christ can do that.

The life that Jesus gave was an offering, which is a sacrificial offering and a sacrifice, which is the act of offering. So basically, He just didn't talk about it; He did it. His body was the sacrifice, and the act of offering was on the cross. And it was a well-pleasing odor to God; that is, it was a sweet smell. The priests would offer some of the sacrifices by fire, and that would be a sweet-smelling aroma to God (Lev. 1). What made the death of Christ sweet to God was that He fulfilled the law.

"But fornication, and all uncleanness, or covetousness, let it not be once named among you, as becometh saints" (Eph. 5:3). Fornication is sexual immorality, which is sex outside of marriage, and it is unlawful according to God's Word. This includes not only the act but also the thoughts. This is one thing that came from the first church council in Jerusalem in Acts 15:20. The legalistic Jews tried to force the Gentiles to be circumcised physically to be saved. But when the church leaders met, James stood up and gave a list of things that the Gentile believers should not be involved in or doing. Paul had a tough time with this with the Corinthians. He mentioned it numerous times in the book of 1 Corinthians. Paul also mentioned this as one of the deeds of the flesh in Galatians 5:19–21. Right after fornication, Paul adds, "and all uncleanness," which is impurity or immorality.

Covetousness is a desire to have more, and it goes with greed. Scripture also has a lot to say about this sin. Thou shalt not covet is one of the Ten Commandments (Exod. 20:17). When a person covets something, that person sets his or her heart on it. Whether it is material things or the neighbor's spouse. It is a desire that makes a person unsatisfied what he or she has. All three of these sins, fornication, uncleanness, and covetousness, let it not once be mentioned in you. It should not be mentioned that you do any of these things. There should not be any room for discussion about whether this is right or wrong for believers.

"As becometh saints" means just as fitting or suitable believers. This means that as believers, these sins are not suitable for who we are in Christ. We are to be distinguished by our lifestyles, and we cannot be distinguished if we commit these sins.

"Neither filthiness, nor foolish talking, nor jesting, which are not convenient: but rather giving of thanks" (Eph. 5:4). The previous verse spoke about the proper behavior of the believer; this verse speaks of the communication of the believer. Filthiness means obscenity, disgrace, or indecency. Foolish talking is talking with vulgar language, jokes, and actions. Jesting is conversation that easily turns vulgar. This means that conversation can turn something said into something perverted. This goes back to Ephesians 4:29, when Paul said let not corrupt communication proceed out of your mouth. That is what these things are: rotten, defiling, disgusting talk. These things are not proper for believers to be saying, which is what Paul means by saying they are not convenient.

Just as certain members of society have things that are considered proper and improper, so does the believer. At a dinner, it is proper for certain people to sit in certain places, it is proper for them to act a certain way, and it is proper for them to eat a certain way with certain utensils. As believers, it is proper for us to talk a certain way. Just as it is proper for men and women to act a certain way, so is it proper for believers. It is not proper for believers to use vulgar language or speak in an indecent way or turn a normal conversation into something perverted. Paul says believers should instead give thanks. Instead of talking like this, believers should be giving glory to God for what He has done. This is the will of God (1 Thess. 5:18).

"For this ye know, that no whoremonger, nor unclean person, nor covetous man, who is an idolater, hath any inheritance in the kingdom of Christ and of God" (Eph. 5:5). For you may be sure of this—that is, you can be guaranteed—that someone who is sexually immoral, any impure person, or anyone who is covetous will not have any portion of the kingdom of Christ and of God. Paul said the same things to the Corinthians (1 Cor. 6:9–10) and to the Galatians (Gal. 5:21). The writer of Hebrews said that whoremongers and adulterers God will judge (Heb. 13:4). Paul said the covetous person is an idolater, which means the person who is greedy to have more worships the things he or she is after. The kingdom of Christ and of God shows the oneness of the Father and Son. The kingdom belongs to both.

"Let no man deceive you with vain words: for because of these things cometh the wrath of God upon the children of disobedience" (Eph. 5:6). Paul warns the Ephesians to let no man cheat them with empty words. Don't let people who live in these sins cheat you with words that have no truth in them. They don't believe the previous verse, so they will convince themselves and others that that is not the case with people who commit those sins. Do not let them cheat you with claims that are not true. Because of these sins, the wrath of God comes upon them. They will try to deny the wrath of God coming on them. They will try to deny that they will not be allowed into the kingdom of God. Not only do they not have any portion in the kingdom of God, but the wrath of God is also coming on them, they who are children of unbelief. God will punish them because of their unbelief. These sinful unbelievers will cheat themselves and others with their lies. Paul wrote to the Galatians, "Be not deceived; God is not mocked: for whatsoever a man soweth, that shall he also reap" (Gal. 6:7). And again, remember it says in Ephesians 2:2–3 that we were once unbelievers, children of disobedience, but through the death of Christ, we were made alive in Him. This deception that God's wrath will not come upon sinners is still around today. They are cheating themselves and others with this deception.

"Be not ye partakers with them" (Eph. 5:7). This means do not become partners with them. Do not participate with them in their sins. Why? Because of the coming punishment upon the children of unbelief. The Ephesians do not want to be a partner with someone knowing God will judge him or her. They will try to cheat the Ephesians by lying to them about their sins and try to convince them that it is okay. Paul warns the Ephesians not to participate with them in their sins. Why would believers want to partner with men and women in their sins knowing that God's wrath will come upon him or her?

"For ye were sometimes darkness, but now are ye light in the Lord: walk as children of light" (Eph. 5:8). Notice Paul did not say that they were in the darkness but that they *were* darkness. This darkness does not refer to things like witchcraft or satanic things. But living in sin is darkness, no matter what the sin is. That sounds dreadful, to know that living in sin is darkness. We can go back and read Ephesians 2:11–12 and 4:18, where Paul reminds us of who we were before Christ. When Paul said they were once darkness, he is referencing their past lifestyles. Again, Gentile means non-Jew, but it also means unbelievers. Paul is saying they were sinful men and women.

Paul says you are light in the Lord. Notice, he didn't say you are in the light. They have been enlightened, that is spiritually illuminated. Paul is making a contrast between light and darkness. When it is dark, you cannot see anything, and so it is when you are in sin. When you live in sin, which is darkness, you don't know that the wrong you do is sin; you just think it is okay. But when it is light, you see things you would have stumbled over in the dark. So it is when you are light in the Lord; you see the things you did as a sinner as sinful. When the Ephesians became believers, they were no longer darkness. It says in John 1:4–5 that life is in Jesus and the life is the light of men and this light shines in the darkness. In John 1:9, the true Light lights every man that comes into the world. Jesus said, "I am come a light into the world, that whosoever believeth on Me should not abide in darkness" (John 12:46). Jesus also told His disciples, "I am the light of the world: he that followeth Me shall not walk in darkness, but shall have the light of life" (John 8:12).

Jesus is the life and the light. He is the light that shines on our sin. When we live in sin, we are dead, and Paul already made that clear in Ephesians chapter 2. If we believe in Jesus as our Lord and Savior, then we have the light and life. Believers will not remain in darkness, which is sin. People who remain in their sin do not have the light and do not have the life. You cannot be light and darkness at the same time. In other words, you cannot be a believer and remain in your sin. Light and darkness cannot occupy the same space. Paul mentions this in 2 Corinthians 6:14: "Be ye not unequally yoked together with unbelievers: for what fellowship hath righteousness with unrighteousness? And what communion hath light with darkness?" He continues with light and dark into 2 Corinthians 7:1.

Paul has reminded them of their past lifestyles so that they would remember who they were before Christ and hopefully to keep them from falling back into that same sinful life. This is written for us, too, to keep us from making that decision to return to our past sinful lifestyles. Paul tells them to walk as children of light. In other words, live differently, just as the difference between light and dark. People should be able to see a difference between believers and unbelievers.

"For the fruit of the Spirit is in all goodness and righteousness and truth" (Eph. 5:9). This verse can be translated as "the fruit of the light." Basically, since believers are light, their works should demonstrate it. "The fruit of the Spirit is love, joy, peace, longsuffering, gentleness, goodness, faith, meekness, temperance: against such there is no law" (Gal. 5:22–23). So, believers who are the light have the work of the Spirit or light, which is in all goodness, integrity, and truth. These should be within the work of all believers.

"Proving what is acceptable unto the Lord" (Eph. 5:10). This is testing to approve what is well pleasing to the Lord. Basically, the idea is to question whether something pleases God. This goes for any area of life. Matthew Henry wrote that we must not only dread and avoid that which is displeasing to God, but we should inquire and consider what will be acceptable to Him[3]. That means a believer should question whether something he or she is contemplating or presently doing lines up with what Paul has just written in the previous verses. Does the believer's life line up with how a believer is supposed to behave and talk?

"And have no fellowship with the unfruitful works of darkness,

---

[3] Matthew Henry 1662-1712, Matthew Henry's Commentary volume 3 (London, 1845; public domain)

but rather reprove them" (Eph. 5:11). To have no fellowship with them means not to partner or associate with them. Earlier Paul said not to partake with those who live in sin. This does not mean we have to live in a cave somewhere, but it does mean that we are not to join in with them or participate in their sins. Remember, it is not fitting for believers to sin, and it shouldn't be mentioned that they do. When a believer partners with the unfruitful works of darkness, he or she is not living as a believer. Paul called it the unfruitful works of darkness, meaning barren, unable to bear fruit. The works of darkness do not produce anything helpful to anybody. This is another contrast between believers and unbelievers. Believers' works are fruitful, and the works of darkness are unfruitful. The question to ask is when someone lived in sin, did any good come of it? What came out of our lives of sin?

A psalmist wrote, "Blessed is the man that walketh not in the counsel of the ungodly, nor standeth in the way of sinner, nor sitteth in the seat of the scornful. But his delight is in the law of the LORD; and in His law doth he meditate day and night" (Ps. 1:1–2). How happy is the man who lives not in the purpose of the wicked? How happy is the man who does not establish or settle in the habit of sinners? How happy is the man who is not resolved to sit in the seat of mockers? Solomon said, "Enter not into the path of the wicked, and go not in the way of evil men. Avoid it, pass not by it, turn from it, and pass away" (Pro. 4:14–15). Paul wrote to the Romans, the Corinthians, the Thessalonians, and Timothy to turn from such people (Rom. 16:17; 1 Cor. 5:9–11; 1 Cor. 10:2–21; 2 Cor. 6:14–18; 2 Thess. 3:6, 14; 1 Tim. 6:5; 2 Tim. 3:5).

To reprove is to convict or expose. We reprove them not by protesting or judging them, and we do not talk about their lifestyles before others, which Paul will discuss in the next verse. We convict them, or expose their sin, by talking to them one-on-one, and we convict them by our lifestyle. That is why believers are not to live in sin or participate with them who do. We cannot expose and convict them if we are guilty of participating or partnering in their sins.

Paul says, "for it is a shame even to speak of those things which are done of them in secret" (Eph. 5:12). The sins that people commit in secret are shameful for believers to even talk about. So basically, if we hear or see someone living a life of sin, it is not our responsibility to tell the neighbor or our friend; we are to talk with that person and reprove him or her if that person comes around us. Our lifestyle should be such that they are convicted. It is a shame to speak of the sin when others are not ashamed to live in it. And since it is not proper to talk filthy, it should be a shame for believers to talk about the sin that others commit.

"But all things that are reproved are made manifest by the light: for whatsoever doth make manifest is light" (Eph. 5:13). All things that have been exposed are made known by the light. It is light that reveals and light that makes everything known. Light shines on things that are not seen in the dark. It exposes things so that they will be known. The sins that men live will be known and exposed by the light, either by the Word of God or by the life of believers. "Wherefore He saith, awake thou that sleepest, and arise from the dead, and Christ shall give thee light" (Eph. 5:14). This refers to the ones who are spiritually asleep, the ones whose sins have been discovered by the light. It is time to get up and do something about it. Repentance is to what Paul is referring. Now since you have been found out, it is time to repent of your sins. This may have been an Easter hymn as an invitation to unbelievers. Sinner are asleep and dead (Eph. 2:5). When they wake and arise and repent of their sins, Christ will shine upon them. This is a wakeup call for all who are living in sin. This should be an encouragement for the sinner to turn to Christ and from his sin.

"See then that ye walk circumspectly, not as fools, but as wise" (Eph. 5:15). Since the believer tries to reprove the sinner, the believer needs to be careful in how he or she lives. Paul is telling believers to see to it that they walk exactly, correctly, and carefully. They are to pay attention to how they live. He says not as fools, which are people who lack sense or wisdom. Someone who lacks sense does not pay attention to what he or she is doing or how he or she is living. These types of people don't consider on how their lives affect others. But the wise will see that they walk carefully so that they don't look like hypocrites. The wise will live as believers should and will talk as proper believers. The wise walk carefully, or exactly, so that their lives will reprove the lives of sinners. The wise will not participate in the sins of darkness.

Solomon said, "Keep thy heart with all diligence; for out of it are the issues of life. Put away from thee a froward mouth, and perverse lips put far from thee. Let thine eyes look right on, and let thine eyelids look straight before thee. Ponder the path of thy feet, and let all thy ways be established. Turn not to the right hand nor to the left: remove thy foot from evil" (Prov. 4:23–27). Solomon is saying protect the heart because that is the seat of our emotions. Out of the heart comes the source, or springs, of life. Put off a perverse mouth and talk. Keep your eyes focused, consider the path of your feet, and let all your ways be fixed, or sure.

"Redeeming the time, because the days are evil" (Eph. 5:16). Redeeming the time means buying up every opportunity. It means to use every opportunity to live exactly or correctly. It means living in a way so that no one can accuse the believer of hypocrisy. Picture a merchant taking the opportunity to buy up things needed for his business. So the believer needs to be taking the opportunity to live his or her life for Christ. Not being foolish, wasting opportunities, or participating in the sins of others, but being wise and living exactly, because the wise know the days are evil. There is enough evil in the world without the believer adding to it by being foolish and not paying attention to how he or she lives. The days are evil, meaning we are surrounded by sinful people, and we are to buy up every opportunity to live exactly.

"Wherefore be ye not unwise, but understanding what the will of the Lord is" (Eph. 5:17). To be unwise is to be ignorant, and to be ignorant is to not know. So basically, Paul is telling the Ephesians not to be ignorant but to fully grasp the Lord's purpose. Paul is telling the Ephesians this so they would know. Paul is telling them what the will of the Lord is, which includes living carefully, redeeming the time, and a few more actions that will be covered in the next few verses. The will of God is not something mysterious or something they must keep searching for. God revealed His will, which also includes for all men to be saved (1 Tim. 2:4); to be pure (1 Thess. 4:3); and to be thankful (1 Thess. 5:18). God does not leave us clueless in what He desires for our lives. But God does give us the desires of our hearts (Ps. 37:4). That does not mean that God will give us whatever we desire, but it does mean that God gives us a desire to do what He would have us do.

"And be not drunk with wine, wherein is excess; but be filled with the Spirit" (Eph. 5:18). We all know what being drunk with wine does to a person. Drunken people are controlled by the wine, which is called spirits. Paul says being drunk with wine is excess, which is to be extremely indulgent. The word *excess* is also called riot, which refers to wild parties and things like that. Drunken people sometimes act differently than when they are sober, and sometimes the wine makes a person act worse than he or she normally acts. People who are drunk are usually an embarrassment to themselves and the people around them. Scripture has a lot to say about being drunk, including some examples (Gen. 9:21; Gen. 19:32–35; Prov. 20:1; Prov. 23:20–21; Rom. 13:13; 1 Cor. 6:10; Gal. 5:21).

Paul tells them instead of being drunk with wine, which they probably experienced during their time as unbelievers, be filled with the Holy Spirit. The Holy Spirit fills the believer at the time of salvation. To be filled with the Holy Spirit means to allow Him to work in our lives. It means to live as God would have us live, according to His Word.

"Speaking to yourselves in psalms and hymns and spiritual songs, singing and making melody in your heart to the Lord" (Eph. 5:19). "Speaking to yourselves" does not mean to talk to yourself. It means to talk to one another. This means they are to be together singing psalms, hymns, and spiritual songs. They are to come together and build one another up in song. There is something about a song that can change a person's mood. Psalms are songs with music, referring to the book of Psalms. Hymns are probably only Christian; different from the Psalms, a hymn is a song of praise to God. Spiritual songs are songs sung by spiritual persons, praising God or Christ and possibly testifying to God's grace.

Singing in praise to God and making melody also mean to sing praise with music. You can sing along with music or not; either way, you can sing praises to God. Paul is making a contrast between people drunk with wine and believers filled with the Holy Spirit. Usually drunks sing songs that are not morally fit and should not be uttered, while Spirit-filled believers sing songs praising God.

"Giving thanks always for all things unto God and the Father in the name of our Lord Jesus Christ" (Eph. 5:20). The Spirit-filled believer will give thanks to God. As mentioned earlier, it is God's will for the believer to be giving thanks to God. The believer should be giving thanks at all times for everything unto God. Giving thanks should keep us from complaining about our circumstances. Remember, Paul was in prison, yet he wrote giving thanks always for everything. We thank God, who is the Father, in the name of our Lord Jesus Christ.

"Submitting yourselves one to another in the fear of God" (Eph. 5:21). Spirit-filled believers will line up under one another, which means they will submit. It is to know who is in authority over us and to submit under them. When Paul says "in the fear of God," he is referring to a reverential fear of displeasing God. Everything we do should honor God, and if we submit to another, then we do it to please God. We can read Romans 13:1–5; Hebrews 13:17; and 1 Peter 2:13, 5.5 about submitting to authorities. Paul talks more about submission in the next set of verses going into Ephesians chapter 6.

"Wives, submit yourselves unto your own husbands, as unto the Lord" (Eph. 5:22). Paul begins with wives submitting to their husbands. It could be addressing wives who have been disrespectful or unruly toward their husbands. In our culture today, we see unruly and disrespectful wives, but it shouldn't be that way with the Spirit-filled wife. Submission is to voluntarily line up under someone, and that someone to the wife is her husband. It is to know who is the authority and to line up under that authority. Just because wives submit to their husbands does not mean that they should lose their self-respect. Husbands, just because our wives are to submit to us does not mean we rule our houses with iron fists or treat them as if they are unworthy and undeserving. Just because Paul deals with wives first does not mean he has nothing to say to husbands. In fact, Paul has more to say to husbands than he does to wives.

Wives, the call to submit to your own husbands means that you line up under your husbands' authority and not the authority of another woman's husband. In other words, let's say a wife and husband have discussed something for which the wife was seeking a response. The husband gives the final answer. The wife submits to her own husband by subjecting to his authority. This does not mean the wife goes to talk to another man to get a different response than her husband gave. The wife must submit to her own husband, and no other man has the authority to give the wife a different response than what her husband gave. The only time the wife submits to another man is if he is in the place of authority as far as the workplace or in some other kind of leadership role.

Remember, this is the Spirit-filled or believing wife. Paul says to submit to your husbands as unto the Lord; that is, Jesus Christ. Submit to your own husbands as you submitted to the Lord. When the wife submits to the Lord as her Lord and Savior, she in honor to her Lord and Savior also submits to her own husband. God has set the husband to be the head of the wife, as stated in Genesis 3:16. If the husband is an unbeliever, the same applies as Peter said in 1 Peter 3:1–6.

"For the husband is the head of the wife" (Eph. 5:23). This is the reason for the wife's submission to her husband. The husband being the head of the wife means that he is the authority. The husband does not tell his wife this or force her to submit. As a Spirit-filled believer, she submits to her husband to honor her Lord. A dictator forces people to submit, but the wife submits because of her love for Jesus Christ and in obedience to the Word.

"Even as Christ is head of the church: and He is the saviour of the body" (Eph. 5:23). In Ephesians 1:22–23, Paul already made it clear that Jesus is the head of the church. God the Father placed Him as the head, so Paul uses Jesus as an example of how the husband is the head of the wife. The church is made up of the believers in Jesus Christ. As Christ is the authority of the church, He is the deliverer of the body, which is the church. This is not to say that the husband can deliver his wife from her sins, but it is an example of Jesus's love for the church. He is protecting and providing. The example is that the husband is to be the protector and provider for the wife and so she should submit to him.

"Therefore as the church is subject unto Christ, so let the wives be to their own husbands in everything" (Eph. 5:24). Just as the church has lined up under the authority of Christ, so let the wives do to their own husbands. The church is the individual believers, which include the husband, and just as the believer is subject to Christ, so let the wives be to their husbands. In everything means just that. The believing wife honors the Lord when she submits to her husband.

"Husbands, love your wives, even as Christ also loved the church, gave Himself for it (Eph. 5:25). Paul has more to say to the husbands because more responsibility falls on them. Jesus loved the church, and

He demonstrated it by giving Himself for it. This is for the Spirit-filled husband. To love someone is to make them feel important, or to make much of someone. Paul is telling husbands that to love their wives is to make them feel important. It is to do things for their wives' benefit. This is what the husband is to do for his wife, not another woman. The husband is not to make another woman feel important; neither is the other woman to take the place of the wife. Paul wrote to the Colossians, "Husbands, love your wives, and be not bitter against them" (Col. 3:19). This means do not be angered toward her. Peter wrote, "Likewise, ye husbands, dwell with them according to knowledge, giving honour unto the wife, as unto the weaker vessel, and as being heirs together of the grace of life; that your prayers be not hindered" (1 Pet. 3:7). Live with her according to knowledge, esteeming and showing dignity to her, as unto the weaker vessel, knowing that the wife is not like the husband. God created her different, and it is wrong to treat her as if she were built like a man. Also, realize that she is also heir with you in eternal life. If you treat her right, your prayers will not be cut out or interrupted; that is, they will not be unanswered. Loving your wife will keep her from seeing her submission to you as degrading.

Jesus gave His life for the church. Again, this is not to say that the husband can save his wife from her sins, but the husband is to love his wife so much that he is willing to give up his life for her. Jesus gave His life as an offering and a sacrifice for the church (Eph. 5:2), and the example Paul lays out for the husband is to offer and sacrifice his life for his wife. This does not mean that the husband sacrifices his life so that she can have all the comforts of life. But it does mean that he might have to die to protect her and do without to provide for her needs.

Another question might come up: What if the wife is an unbeliever? The answer is that the husband is to love her as Christ loved the church and gave His life for it. Remember, Paul is writing to Spirit-filled husbands. Paul dealt with this in 1 Corinthians 7:12–14, which goes for the wife as well.

"That He might sanctify and cleanse it with the washing of water by the word" (Eph. 5:26). In this verse, Paul is referring to the church. Sanctify means to set apart, to separate. Cleanse means to make clean. Washing of water refers to bathing, not salvation by baptism. That is,

Paul is saying that the church is set apart and made clean by the Word of God. So just as a person is made physically clean by bathing, the soul is made clean by the Word of God.

"That He might present it to Himself a glorious church, not having spot, or wrinkle, or any such thing; but that it should be holy and without blemish" (Eph. 5:27). Jesus sanctified and cleansed the church so that He Himself could present the church as radiant, without any defilement, flaw, or anything of the sort. This is when the church, or the believers, stand before Him on that final day. The church, or believers, should be set apart and faultless. The blood of Christ made us faultless, and the Word of God has made us clean.

"So ought men to love their wives as their own bodies. He that loveth his wife loveth himself. For no man ever yet hated his own flesh; but nourisheth and cherisheth it, even as the Lord the church" (Eph. 5:28–29). The word *ought* means that it makes the husband a debtor. It is to owe; it is obligatory to love his wife. The church is the body of Christ. Jesus demonstrated His love for His body by giving His life for it in order that He might present it Himself a radiant church, without any defilement, flaw, or anything of the sort. And so, the husband is obligated to demonstrate his love for his wife by giving his life for her, keeping her from anything that would defile her, setting her apart as his wife and no other woman. How the husband loves his body, not in a selfish kind of way but loving as in taking care of it, is how he should treat his wife. The husband strengthens and takes care of his body. The reference is just as Christ loved His body and did these things, so should the husband love his body, which is his wife, and he should follow the example of Jesus. He who loves his wife loves his body.

"For we are members of His body, of His flesh, and of His bones" (Eph. 5:30). Paul is referring to the church and Jesus Christ and the husband and the wife. The church is the body of Christ and because He loves the church, He will take care of it and provide for it. And so, since the wife is part of the husband, part of his body, he is to take care of her and provide for her, just as he does for his body.

"For this cause shall a man leave his father and mother, and shall be joined unto his wife, and they two shall be one flesh" (Eph. 5:31). Paul is quoting Genesis 2:24. Because the wife is part of the husband, they are now to leave behind their mothers and fathers. In other words, they are to branch out on their own and start their own family. The husband shall be joined to his wife means just as glue sticks two things together and cannot be taken apart without tearing, so are the husband and wife to be glued together. What God has joined together, let no man tear asunder, as the minister says during a wedding ceremony. Jesus quoted Genesis also in Matthew 19:5.

"This is a great mystery: but I speak concerning Christ and the church. Nevertheless let everyone of you in particular so love his wife even as himself; and the wife see that she reverence her husband" (Eph. 5:32–33). This is something that God has hidden but revealed to Paul. God revealed to Paul the connection between Jesus and the church and the husband and the wife. Let each one of you separately love his wife as you do your body. Paul is speaking to each individual husband and telling him to love his wife, not to love another man's wife as you would your wife. Each husband is to love you wife, make her feel important, try your best to protect her well-being, and do not let anything defile her. Wives, see that you honor and respect your own husband and not another woman's husband.

Ephesians Chapter 6

Chapter 6 of the book of Ephesians continues the discussion of Spirit-filled believers' conduct, including children and fathers (parents) and servants and masters in verses 1–9 and believer's warfare in verses 10–20. Final greetings are given in verses 21–24.

"Children, obey your parents in the Lord: for this is right" (Eph. 6:1). The word *obey* means to listen attentively, to heed, and to conform to authority. Children and servants, which we will get to later, are to be obedient to parents and masters. Paul does not say submit, but submission is implied. If you refuse to obey the authoritative persons in your life, you will not submit to them. Submission is needed in obedience.

We are still talking about Spirit-filled people. Spirit-filled wives submit to their husbands; Spirit-filled husbands love their wives; and Spirit-filled children obey their parents. The age or gender of the child does not matter; they are to listen to and heed their parents if they live under their roof. We can go back to Ephesians 5:31: when the child leaves the home and marries, then the child is free from obeying his or her parents. But if they still live at home, even in their twenties, thirties, or later, they must heed their parents' rules. Children, obey your parents is what Paul wrote and not the other way around. In today's time, it is typical to see parents obeying the children.

Children, obey your parents in the Lord, for this is what is right. In other words, children are to obey their parents as they obey and submit to the Lord Jesus Christ. The only time a child should not obey his or her parents is if it contradicts the Word of God. Proverbs 1:8 reads, "My son, hear the instruction of thy father, and forsake not the law of thy mother." This means to listen attentively to the correction or discipline of your father and not to reject the statute of your mother. Proverbs 6:20 reads, "My son, keep thy father's commandments, and forsake not the law of thy mother." To keep is to maintain, and to maintain is to continue something; that something is his father's commandment. Proverbs 23:22 reads, "Hearken unto thy father that begat thee, and despise not thy mother when she is old."

"Honour thy father and mother; which is the first commandment with promise;" (Eph. 6:2). There is a difference between obeying and honoring. Obeying your parents is while you are still living at home. Honoring your parents is for life. They will always be your parents, no matter what. If they disown you, they are still your parents, and we are to honor them as such. To honor is to respect them. Honoring your mother and father is not the first commandment, but it is the first to give a promise. "Honour thy father and mother: that thy days may be long upon the land which the LORD thy God giveth thee" (Exod. 20:12). Deuteronomy 27:16 reads, "Cursed be he that setteth light by his father or his mother. And all the people shall say, Amen." This means the person who dishonors or despises his mother or father is to be cursed. Proverbs 20:20 says, "Whoso curseth his father or his mother, his lamp shall be put out in obscure darkness." This means that person will not be remembered.

Here is the promise: "that it may be well with thee, and thou mayest live long on the earth" (Eph. 6:3). Does this mean that a person will live long? No, but it should put us in the frame of mind to always honor our parents. Just because children die in their youth does not mean they dishonored their parents. The same goes for people who live to be 110; it doesn't mean they always honored their parents. Honor your parents in order that good will come to pass and that you may live long—that is, a long time on the earth. Paul is quoting from Deuteronomy: "Honour thy father and thy mother, as the LORD thy God commanded thee; that thy days may be prolonged, and that it may go well with thee, in the land which the LORD thy God giveth thee" (5:16). When God gave this command to the children of Israel, they were going to the promised land. So basically, they would live long in the land that God was giving them. Paul says we need to honor our parents so that we may live long on the earth. Paul knew that the promise made to the Israelites was for them only, but the promise of living long applies to everybody. We honor our parents as long as they are living, and honoring them means more than respect; it includes taking care of them when the time comes.

"And, ye fathers, provoke not your children to wrath: but bring them up in the nurture and admonition of the Lord" (Eph. 6:4). Paul does not leave his instruction one sided. He didn't tell the wives to submit to their husbands without telling the husbands to love their wives. He did not tell the children to obey their parents without telling the parents not to provoke their children to anger. It is thought that Paul is talking to both parents and not just fathers. In the first verse Paul told children to obey their parents. But he could just be referring to the fathers because the responsibility of the family falls more on the father.

Provoke not your children to wrath means don't make them angry. Don't get to the point where the children are angry because of the way you treated them. In Colossians 3:21, Paul said to the fathers, "Do not provoke your children to anger, lest they be discouraged." This is not talking about rules, standards, or what is expected of the child. This refers to things that would drive a child to be furious at his or her parents. Overbearing actions, constant negativity, neglect, and comparison are just a few. The reason Paul said fathers instead of parents could be the father is more prone to anger the child more than the mother. But the mother can be just as bad as, or even worse than, the father. But since Paul told the children to obey their parents, he is probably referring to both mother and father.

To bring them up is to nourish them. It is the same word as nourish in Ephesians 5:29. This means that fathers are to bring up their children to maturity. That means to make them healthy and strong. Just as the husband is to nourish his wife, he is also to nourish his children. The father is to nourish the children in the discipline and correction of the Lord. This means that Spirit-filled believers who are led by the Lord are to nourish and discipline their children according to the Word of God.

We are to teach our children the Word of God (Deut. 6:7; 11:19–21); we are to share what God has done in our lives (Josh. 4:6–7, 21–24); we are to let our children know whom we worship (Josh. 24:15), meaning take a stand for Christ; we are to pass on to the next generation what God has done (Ps. 78:4–7); we are to tell them the laws and commandments (Prov. 4:1–4). How can children know how to behave if their parents do not instruct them?

Scripture also speaks about disciplining our children. Disciplining our children corrects and instructs them (Prov. 19:18; 22:15; 23:13–14; 29:15). We are not to abuse our children, which will provoke them to anger, but discipline is necessary for correction. There are many ways to discipline our children. What works for one child may not work for another, but we cannot neglect disciplining our children. It is up to us to discipline our children and to know what will break them from disobedience. It is our job to raise our children, not the job of the school system, the justice system, the government, or any other parent. Children need to go to school to learn the requirements of life, but to be mature adults, they need to learn from their parents how to live.

We are to nourish them in the admonition, which is a mild rebuke or warning of the Lord. This means to encourage or correct them by word, to explain to them what they have done wrong. This is also done from the Word of God. Fathers and mothers have so much on their shoulders. As Spirit-filled parents, we are to bring our children up in the training and admonition of the Lord, meaning we are to follow the Word of God in bringing them up. Children are given to us by God, and it is our responsibility to teach them—including punishment—to bring them to maturity. The Geneva Bible Translation notes have this to say: it is the duty of the fathers to use their fatherly authority moderately and to God's glory[4]. In other words, fathers, do not abuse your authority. You are to lovingly be the head of your wife and the loving authority figure in your home.

"Servants, be obedient to them that are your masters according to the flesh" (Eph. 6:5). Servants are ones who are in subjection; they are men and women of servile condition. Even though we are not servants in a slavelike way, we are servants when it comes to subjection to our masters, who are our supervisors. The term *obedient* here is the same as in verse 1, and it means to listen attentively and heed authority, and it includes submission. Masters are in the authority position. This verse is directed at Spirit-filled servants. Even though they are free in Christ,

---

[4] Geneva Bible Translation Notes, 1599 Geneva Bible Translation Notes

they are still to obey their masters. Paul added "according to the flesh," which means according to the physical, and it means to line up under the authority.

"With fear and trembling, in singleness of your heart, as unto Christ" (Eph. 6:5). This fear is a good type of fear; it is a fear of displeasing the masters. Trembling is quaking, and singleness is sincerity of the heart. Basically, this verse is saying, obey your masters with fear of displeasing them and with quaking, knowing that there will be consequences if you don't obey them with sincerity, or honesty. Paul said the same thing to the Colossians: "Servants, obey in all things your masters according to the flesh; not with eye service, as men pleasers; but in singleness of heart, fearing God" (Col. 3:22). We can also read in 1 Timothy 6:1–2 and Titus 2:9–10 about being in submission to our masters. Peter tells us to be subject to our master with all fear, not only to the good and gentle but also to the crooked (1 Pet. 2:18).

"As unto Christ" means in the manner as you would toward Christ. The same way we are obedient to our Lord is the same way we are to be obedient to our masters, with fear and trembling and sincerity of the heart.

"Not with eyeservice, as men pleasers; but as the servants of Christ, doing the will of God from the heart" (Eph. 6:6). Eye service means being obedient only when being watched. Men pleasers refers to pleasing a man, trying to win approval from him. To be obedient with fear and trembling and with sincerity of the heart means that you are obedient even when your supervisor is not watching. This means the Spirit-filled servant is being always obedient. Paul reminds us that as the servants of Christ, we are doing the will of God from the heart, meaning the will of God is for us to be always obedient to our masters. The desire of God is for us to be obedient to our masters from the soul. Everything we do should please the Lord. Doing the will of God from the soul is to do His will with everything in us, giving Him our all, including at work. Paul said, "Whatsoever ye do, do it heartily, as unto the Lord, and not unto men" (Col. 3:23). Everything the believer does, he or she should do it from the soul as unto the Lord and not unto men. We are serving the Lord, not man.

"With good will doing service, as to the Lord, and not unto men"

(Eph. 6:7). With kindness, we should perform the duty of a servant as to the Lord and not unto men. Again, we are serving the Lord and not man, and this should keep us from complaining about our jobs. Paul says "with kindness doing service," meaning we should be kind to our masters even if we don't agree with them or we are not being treated fairly. We serve the Lord in sincerity, or honesty. We please Him by being always obedient. So we serve with kindness as unto the Lord. An example of this is Jacob in Genesis chapter 31. A good message to listen to is Adrian Rogers's "Turning the Rat Race into a Pilgrimage."

"Knowing that whatsoever good thing any man doeth, the same shall be receive of the Lord, whether he be bond or free" (Eph. 6:8). If the believer is doing the duty of a servant to the Lord, we should know that whatsoever good thing we do, the same we shall receive of the Lord. God will reward us for being obedient and doing our duty with kindness and sincerity. We may not receive anything from our masters for following the will of God, but we will receive good things from the Lord for our obedience to Him. If we do our jobs grudgingly, then we do them grudgingly to the Lord. Whether a person is a slave or free, if a man does what he is supposed to do, the Lord will reward him. And the free man is the master; Paul talks about him next.

"And, ye masters, do the same things unto them, forbearing threatening: knowing that your Master also is in heaven; neither is there respect of persons with Him" (Eph. 6:9). Again, we are talking about the Spirit-filled person. Here, Paul is talking to the Spirit-filled master. Just as the servant is to respect his master, the master is to respect his servant. Masters are to give the servants what is due to them. Notice that the servant or employee cannot demand more from the master; only what the master sees fit is what he or she pays. The Old Testament talks about how masters are to treat their servants or slaves (Lev. 19:13; 25:39–46; Deut. 15:11–16; 24:14–15). There are some additional references in the New Testament about masters' treatment of their servants (Col. 4:1; James 5:4).

Forbearing threatening means to relax on the threats. It is telling them not to be harsh to the servants. The Geneva Bible Translation Notes says it is the duty of masters to use the authority that they have over their servants modestly and in a holy manner, seeing that they in another respect have a common master who is in heaven, who will judge both the servant and the free.[5] God is no respecter of persons, meaning God doesn't play favoritism with men.

"Finally, my brethren, be strong in the Lord, and in the power of His might" (Eph. 6:10). This word *finally* is literally for the rest. This is not necessarily Paul finishing this letter; rather, he is saying the last thing I want to leave you is this. Then he continues with his instruction. Paul did this in his letter to the Corinthians and to the Philippians as well, meaning he is not ending his letter but giving final instructions.

Brethren are believers, and Paul is telling them to be strong in the Lord. Being strong in the Lord is to be strengthened in Him. This is a command, and it is a continuous action, meaning it is something that believers need to constantly be doing. Our strength comes from the Lord Jesus Christ. Paul has already prayed that they would be strengthened in Ephesians 1:19 and 3:16. One was for them to know the power of God, and the other was to be strengthened by His Spirit. So basically, it is to be enabled by strength in the Lord.

Paul tells them to be strengthened in the Lord and in the power of His might. That is, to be strengthened in the strength of His power. We are enabled in the Lord, and we have His strength in action. Our strength comes from Jesus Christ alone and not from any book. Books can give us encouragement and advice to get through a situation, but what happens when the situation happens again? We need to remember what the book suggested, but to draw strength from a book is to strengthen the self, and that won't work for what Paul is about to tell us. Paul commands us to be strengthened in the Lord and in the power of His might. One thing self-help books do is tell us who the enemy is.

Moses told the Israelites not to let their hearts be faint, to fear not, to not tremble, and to not be terrified. He continued, saying the Lord was with them and He would fight for them (Deut. 20:3–4). This was for them to claim the promised land. Joshua was also to be strong and of good courage, and God would be with him (Josh. 1:6–9). David passed on to Solomon to be strong and of good courage and the Lord would be with him (1 Chr. 28:20). Zerubbabel was another person who was told to be strong and the Lord would be with him (Hag. 2:4). Paul told

---

[5] Geneva Bible Translation Notes, 1599 Geneva Bible Translation Notes

the Corinthians, "Watch ye, stand fast in the faith, quit you like men, be strong" (1 Cor. 16:13). Timothy was encouraged to be strong (2 Tim. 2:1). So, when we are strengthened in the Lord, we are courageous to face whatever we are going to face. We cannot fear, tremble, or let our hearts faint. We are commanded to be strong in the Lord, which means to be courageous.

"Put on the whole armour of God, that ye may be able to stand against the wiles of the devil" (Eph. 6:11). This is the second command. We are commanded to put on the whole armor of God, which is every piece designed for each part of the body. The whole armor of God covers the body from head to toe, and the believer needs the whole armor so that he or she will be able to stand against the trickery of the devil. To stand is to be firm or unwavering; that is, we are fixed securely. If the believer is to stand securely, he or she needs to put on the whole armor of God. Paul got this illustration from the Roman soldiers who guarded him. The soldiers would have on the whole armor so that they could stand against their enemies.

Wiles means trickery, enticement, and false representations, meaning something that is distorted or a debased version of something. Satan has a method, following, or pursuing of orderly and technical procedures in handling of someone. Satan is crafty and deceitful. Peter compared Satan to a roaring lion seeking those he may devour (1 Pet. 5:8). The devil walks around his prey like the lion does. That's why Peter tells us to be sober and vigilant, meaning to have a sound mind, a mind that is not cluttered with junk, and to be watchful. A sound mind is a mind that is healthy and sensible. It is a mind filled with clean and pure things.

The word *wiles* is the same Greek word as *lie in wait* in Ephesians 4:14. The wiles of the devil, or Satan, is anything that leads us away from the Word of God, anything that leads us into sin, and anything that distorts truth. Every piece of armor is designed to protect a certain part of the body, and it is designed to protect us from the different weapons Satan uses against us. "The weapons of our warfare are not carnal, but mighty through God to the pulling down of strongholds" (2 Cor. 10:4). Our warfare is not with flesh but spiritual. Our weapons of warfare are powerful through God for the destruction of strongholds, or fortified buildings.

"For we wrestle not against flesh and blood, but against principalities, against powers, against the rulers of the darkness of this world, against spiritual wickedness in high places (Eph. 6:12). To begin with, our strife is not against flesh and blood; that is, our fight is not against people. Even though we are not striving against flesh and blood, Satan uses flesh and blood to strive against us. Wrestling is strife, contention, or struggles, and it's contending until one overcomes the other.

Principalities are the chief rulers; powers are authorities; rulers of the darkness of this world are rulers of the darkness of this present age; and spiritual wickedness is evil intent of the wicked spirits of Satan. These are in high places, which means the heavenly places, the sphere that we cannot see. The evil we see in our time is being ruled by Satan's demons. The darkness refers to the sinfulness of this time in which we are living. Not only do they rule because of our sin, but because God has allowed them to rule. They exercise their hostile authority over the world and in this age.

"Wherefore take unto you the whole armour of God, that ye may be able to withstand in the evil day and having done all, to stand" (Eph. 6:13). The words *take unto you* mean to take up or to use the whole armor of God. We need to use the whole armor of God for what it was designed to do. This is the third command from Paul for the believer in this warfare. There is no turning back, no retreat, and if we do turn back, we didn't follow the command to be strong in the Lord and in the power of His might. Taking the whole armor of God is to take both the defensive and the offensive. Paul lists each piece and what it is designed to do in the next few verses.

Paul commands the believer to use the whole armor of God that we might be able to oppose or resist the devil in the evil day. Opposing or resisting means you are active in the fight. We are constantly fighting against Satan and his evil spirits. The evil day is the day of battle. When Satan attacks, we need to be prepared, and that's why Paul commands us to put on and take unto us the whole armor of God. It is just as a soldier on the battlefield knows he needs to be prepared because he doesn't know when the enemy will attack. The evil day is a day of toiling or working, and that is what Satan and his demons are doing, working constantly against us. Every day is an evil day. We are constantly surrounded by evil, and they are constantly attacking.

Paul says we need to use the whole armor of God so that, having done all, we can stand. Having done all means to accomplish or to work fully or to overcome all. Again, to stand is to be firm and fixed securely. So, if the believer wants to be standing securely, he or she needs to have on the whole armor of God. One missing piece could lead to disaster. The main goal is to stand firm, ready for the next attack, and not be overcome by the enemy. We are not to make any progress in this battle. In other words, there is no city to conquer. But we are being attacked and we are to stand firm to keep from being overcome. If a soldier gets knocked down, he is unable to defend himself from the enemy.

"Stand therefore, having the loins girt about with truth" (Eph. 6:14). This is the third time Paul tells the believer to stand. This also means to stand firm or securely fixed. To stand firm means nothing can bring the believer down. There is nothing the enemy could use that could harm or injure the soldier.

The first on the list of armor is the belt of truth, or truthfulness. The loins are the waist, and it refers to a belt. The belt is what keeps loose clothing from getting in the way during battle. The believer needs to be truthful if he or she is to stand firm. The believer needs to be honest and sincere and cannot be a hypocrite. The believer's life needs to line up with what he or she believes. The wiles of the devil and his demons will bring up the insincere and hypocritical lifestyle of the believer, and if he succeeds, he is already winning. In other words, if the believer will not live truthfully, then what is loose, that which is not tucked away or dealt with, will be in the way during the battle and he or she cannot stand firm.

Stand therefore, "having on the breastplate of righteousness" (Eph. 6:14). The breastplate is what protects the vital organs. It covers the rear and the front of the soldier. The breastplate of righteousness protects the heart, which is the seat of the emotions. Righteousness is the righteousness of Christ. It is His righteousness—that is, justification or a right standing with God—that protects the believer from the condemnation of Satan. Standing firm or securely fixed means having on the breastplate of righteousness. Satan cannot hit the believer's heart because of the righteousness of Christ. That means Satan can't condemn the believer of his past sin when he or she has on the breastplate of righteousness, which means that his or her sins have been forgiven.

Stand therefore, "and your feet shod with the preparation of the gospel of peace" (Eph. 6:15). The Roman soldiers' shoes had metal spikes to give them a solid footing. It kept them from slipping during battle. Paul is saying that the believer needs to have his or her feet in the preparation of the gospel of peace. This means that the preparation of the gospel of peace are the shoes the believer needs to have on. Preparation speaks of readiness or preparedness, the gospel is the good message, and peace is rest. The believer needs to stand firm with his or her feet in the preparedness of the good news of peace. The believer will not slip when he or she has his or her feet in these shoes because the gospel of peace, the good message, or good news, of salvation that brought the believer peace with God. The believer can stand firm when he or she has peace with God.

Stand therefore, "above all, taking the shield of faith, wherewith ye shall be able to quench all the fiery darts of the wicked" (Eph. 6:16). In addition to the armor, the believer is to use the shield. Here the word *take* is the same word as in verse 13, which means to take up and use. The shield is shaped like a door; it was two and a half feet wide by four feet high, and it was made of wood coated with animal skin or leather. The shield was the soldier's chief protection. It was large enough for the soldier to hide behind, and the soldiers would also put their shields together to form a wall or roof. Paul said it is the shield of faith, meaning trust or belief in the Word of God. This is not referring to saving faith but rather faith in the Word of God; it is taking God at his Word.

The shield was made so that it would extinguish the fiery arrows of the enemy. The fiery arrows, when lit, would be fired at the army, and when they hit something, they would set things around the object on fire. But the shield protecting the soldier would extinguish the fire. When Satan shoots his fiery arrows at the believer, the believer will use his shield of faith to put out that fire. Faith in the Word of God will protect him or her. The reason Paul said to use the shield of faith above all is because it is our trust in the Word of God that protects believers from all forms of attacks from the enemy. That's why Bible reading, studying, and memorization are important.

Paul continues: "And take the helmet of salvation" (Eph. 6:17), which protected the soldiers' head, ears, necks, and parts of the face. The enemy would target the head of the soldiers. The word *take* here is a different word that means to receive. In other words, the believer is to receive salvation as the helmet to protect him or her. This does not mean that a person receives salvation at this point. Since Paul is talking to believers, they need to receive the helmet of salvation, which refers to the assurance of salvation or deliverance from the battle. The helmet does not protect the mind from losing knowledge, but it protects the head from the attacks concerning the believers' assurance of their salvation.

Paul called this helmet the hope of salvation (1 Thess. 5:8), which is a confident expectation of salvation or deliverance. It is the confident expectation that the believer will be delivered. Satan tries to discourage and bring doubts in the believer's mind, and if he has succeeded, he has dealt a deadly blow to the believer. The most important piece is salvation because if the believer is to stand firm, he or she needs the assurance of his or her deliverance.

And Paul said to receive "the sword of the Spirit, which is the Word of God" (Eph. 6:17). The sword is the only offensive weapon the believer has. We receive the helmet for the assurance of salvation, and so we receive the sword of the Spirit, which is the Word of God. The Word of God is called the sword of the Spirit because the Holy Spirit inspired men to write God's words. This is an important piece of armor the believer needs to receive. The Word of God is compared to the sword in Hebrews 4:12: "The Word of God is quick, and powerful, and sharper than any twoedged sword, piercing even to the dividing asunder of soul and spirit, and of the joints and marrow, and is a discerner of the thoughts and intents of the heart."

The physical sword can do physical damage, but the Word of God is living, powerful, and sharper than any sword man can make because it pierces the soul and spirit, which the physical sword cannot hit. This is a reference to individual verses that believers remember and the Spirit brings to our remembrance. But the requirement is to regularly store Scripture in our minds. Jesus used individual verses when Satan tempted Him. Jesus said, "it is written," referring to the Old Testament (Matt. 4:4–11). If the believer does not receive the sword, he or she will not last long in the battle. If the believer does not use the Word of God as the sword, then he or she will not be able to stand firm on the day of battle. The believer, when he or she receives the sword, can fight back. No soldier who has received a sword refused to use it when the time came. So, the believer who has received the Word of God should use it when the time comes. When heresy or false teaching comes, it is up to the believer who received a sword, who knows how to wield his or her sword by knowing the Word of God correctly, to use his or her sword to fight back.

"Praying always with all prayer and supplication in the Spirit, and watching thereunto with all perseverance and supplication for all saints" (Eph. 6:18). This is not part of the armor, but it is the believer's attitude for battle. The believer needs to be ready and prepared for battle. Paul says praying through every occasion is the meaning for always. That means in every occasion the believer needs to be praying. Paul said in 1 Thessalonian to "pray without ceasing" (5:17), which means pray without stopping. The apostles prayed continually (Acts 6:4), and the early church prayed continually (Acts 1:14; 12:5). Paul continues with all prayer and supplication in the Spirit. The word *prayer* is more general or devotional. The word *supplication* means requests, and it is more of requesting a need. Praying is communion, meaning speaking to God, spending time in prayer, not making requests; supplication is lifting requests to God.

"In the Spirit" refers to the leading of the Holy Spirit to pray. As Spirit-filled believers, we should always be willing to pray. There should not be a time when we are not spending time with the Lord in prayer. Not only should we spend time in prayer, but we should also be praying when circumstances demand us to pray. The Spirit-filled believer should always be a person of prayer, especially since we are in the battle against Satan and his demons.

As Spirit-filled believers, we should also be alert to pray with persistence, which means continuing to make requests concerning all believers. We should be always praying for one another and lifting each other's requests. Again, prayer is more general, and supplication is specific prayer. Whatever the prayer request is, believers should be alert to those needs and requests and make those requests on others' behalf, and we should not stop until God answers that prayer. This does not mean that we should not stop until God sees things our way; instead it means to pray until God gives us the answer we need. Prayer should always be the first thing we do before we start the day. Prayer should be a priority and not a last resort when we have tried everything else. Prayer should be just as important as talking to other people. Since the day is evil and we are always in the battle, the believer should not go without praying.

"And for me, that utterance may be given unto me, that I may open my mouth boldly, to make known the mystery of the gospel" (Eph. 6:19). Paul asks that in their persistence in prayer for all saints, they include him. Notice Paul does not ask them to pray that he be released from prison. He wants them to pray on his behalf, meaning they are to be in intercessory prayer for him. They are to pray for the benefit of Paul. In their persistence in supplication—that is, requests—Paul is making his request known to them so that they will know what to pray for. Paul made similar requests to other churches (Rom. 15:30; 2 Cor. 1:11; Phil. 1:19; Col. 4:3; 1 Thess. 5:25; 2 Thess. 3:1).

Paul's request is that they would pray for words to be given to him so that in boldly, or bluntly, opening his mouth in freedom, he may make known the mystery, or secret, of the gospel. Paul does not ask them to pray that he will have the boldness to preach the gospel, because that boldness is already there. Instead he asks them to pray that when he opens his mouth in freedom, the words will be given to explain the secret of the gospel. This is the sixth time he has mentioned the word *mystery* in this letter (Eph. 1:9; 3:3–4; 3:9; 5:32). He has been given the revelation of this secret, and he is to share it with others. But he needs the right words to explain this secret to others in a way they can understand, and that is Paul's request to them.

Paul continues, "For which I am an ambassador in bonds: that therein I may speak boldly, as I ought to speak" (Eph. 6:20). An ambassador is a representative of a king of the country that sent him, and the ambassador has a message to give to the land to which he is sent. Paul is the representative of the Lord, sent with the good message, and it's for the sake of the good message that he is in chains. For the gospel's sake Paul is in prison, and it is here that he receives the message that all believers need to know, and he needs the words to make it known to them.

So that in it (the gospel) he may speak freely as it is necessary to speak. Now he has the freedom to speak compared to earlier in his ministry when he was threatened, beaten, and rejected. Now people come to hear him speak, and he prays that when he speaks, he will have the words to say to make known the mystery of the gospel. He knows the mystery, but he needs the words to say to make it known to others in way that others can understand.

"But that ye also may know my affairs, and how I do, Tychicus, a beloved brother and faithful minister in the Lord, shall make known to you all things: whom I have sent unto you for the same purpose, that ye might know our affairs, and that he might comfort your hearts" (Eph. 6:21–22). Paul is sending Tychicus to them so he can deliver this letter, but Paul also wants them to know the things concerning him and how he is doing. He didn't put any details in this letter about how he is doing, other than that he is a prisoner of Jesus Christ and an ambassador in chains. Tychicus is to tell them about his welfare. For example, is he sick, has he been injured, how is the ministry, and whatever Paul didn't need to put into his letters.

Paul describes Tychicus as a beloved brother and faithful minister in the Lord, which means Tychicus was a trusted servant in the Lord. He and Trophimus were from Asia Minor, which is modern-day Turkey, and accompanied Paul on his journey from Macedonia to Jerusalem (Acts 20:4). Trophimus went on with Paul to Jerusalem while Tychicus was left in Asia. Tychicus was with Paul in Rome during his first imprisonment, when he was sent to Ephesus, as mentioned in 2 Timothy 4:12, with the letter to the Ephesians. Tychicus was also sent to Colossae for almost the same reason Paul sent him to Ephesus (Col. 4:7–8).

Paul adds, "whom I sent unto you for the same purpose in order that you will know things concerning us," meaning the others who are with Paul: Tychicus, Aristarchus, Marcus, Epaphroditus, and Timotheus. The purpose for sending Tychicus to Ephesus is so the Ephesians will know the things concerning Paul and the others and to encourage their hearts. They had a concern for Paul. After all, he spent three years with them.

Paul finishes his letter with, "Peace be to the brethren, and love with faith, from God the Father and the Lord Jesus Christ. Grace be with all them that love our Lord Jesus Christ in sincerity. Amen" (Eph. 6:23–24). Paul finishes this letter the same way he began it, which is with peace and grace, which was a normal greeting for people at that time. Peace to the brethren refers to believers in Christ. Peace is rest, and it comes from being reconciled to God through the shed blood of Jesus Christ. Love, faith, and peace come from God the Father and the Lord Jesus Christ. Faith works by love (Gal. 5:6). Love accompanied with faith means they work together. Our love for the brethren comes from God, and it demonstrates that love with faith. Grace is unmerited or undeserved favor, and grace will be with all who love our Lord Jesus Christ without corruptness; that is genuine love for Him. Everything Paul prayed for here, let it be fulfilled in the will of God. And some Bibles have at the end of the letter: "To the Ephesians, written from Rome, by Tychicus."

Printed in the United States
By Bookmasters